WOMAN UP!

Praise for

WOMAN UP!

"Aimee Cohen is empowering and inspiring...WOMAN UP! combines your best girlfriend and an elite career expert—in a powerful, purse-sized package! Aimee's advice is easy to follow and gets results."

—**Teresa Taylor**, author of *The Balance Myth* and former COO, Qwest Communications

"As I was first reading WOMAN UP!, I decided that I would order a printed copy for every female in my organization. By the third chapter, I realized that everyone (including men!) needs to read this book."

—**Suzanne Conrad**, CEO, Iowa Donor Network

"WOMAN UP! will be mandatory reading for my 10-year-old daughter. The females in my generation need to be clear and supportive, and provide our wisdom and insights to help women at all levels succeed. WOMAN UP! is a great contribution to help women move forward in whatever career they choose!"

—**Margo Karsten**, CEO,
Cheyenne Regional Medical Center

WOMAN UP!

Overcome the 7 Deadly Sins
that SABOTAGE *Your Success*

AIMEE COHEN

New York

WOMAN UP!
Overcome the 7 Deadly Sins that SABOTAGE *Your Success*

Published in New York, New York, by Morgan James Publishing. Morgan James and The Entrepreneurial Publisher are trademarks of Morgan James, LLC. www.MorganJamesPublishing.com

The Morgan James Speakers Group can bring authors to your live event. For more information or to book an event visit The Morgan James Speakers Group at www.TheMorganJamesSpeakersGroup.com.

ISBN 978-1-63047-192-7 paperback
ISBN 978-1-63047-193-4 eBook
ISBN 978-1-63047-194-1 hardcover
Library of Congress Control Number: 2014935531

A FREE eBook edition is available with the purchase of this print book

CLEARLY PRINT YOUR NAME IN THE BOX ABOVE
Instructions to claim your free eBook edition:
1. Download the BitLit app for Android or iOS
2. Write your name in UPPER CASE in the box
3. Use the BitLit app to submit a photo
4. Download your eBook to any device

Author Photographs by:
Darcy Sherman
www.sassafraspics.com

Cover Design by:
Rachel Lopez
www.r2cdesign.com

Interior Design by:
Bonnie Bushman
bonnie@caboodlegraphics.com

In an effort to support local communities, raise awareness and funds, Morgan James Publishing donates a percentage of all book sales for the life of each book to Habitat for Humanity Peninsula and Greater Williamsburg.

Get involved today, visit
www.MorganJamesBuilds.com.

Habitat
for Humanity®
Peninsula and
Greater Williamsburg
Building Partner

To P…
My love, my heart, my soul

and to Zachary and Rachel
Do what you love, love what you do

CONTENTS

WOMAN UP! *Tips…*

Preface
BIG-GIRL PANTIES

"There is a special place in hell for women who don't help other women."

—Madeleine Albright

What do you want to be when you grow up? It's a question we are all asked as little girls, and we are encouraged to dream big. Fortunately, today, we can be ballerinas, astronauts, doctors, lawyers, executives, and presidents. But no one ever asks you "how" you're going to get there. No one ever tells you how to overcome the self-sabotaging behaviors that get in your way, kill your confidence, and destroy your dreams. Until now.

I may not be an official card-carrying, bra-burning type of feminist, but I believe with every fiber of my being that women are powerful beyond measure, and I have dedicated my career to helping women realize and reach their full professional potential.

As a career coach for more than 20 years, I have worked with and listened to hundreds of women share their stories, their challenges, and their insecurities. I recognize that not only are there external obstacles to a woman's success—such as women only making $0.77 on the dollar, the proverbial "glass ceiling", and the inequities that exist in traditionally male-dominated industries—but there are also internal, self-imposed barriers to overcome. Women unknowingly and unintentionally hold themselves back by engaging in sinful, career-limiting, self-sabotaging behavior.

The truth is that, as women, we already have so much in our favor. We have the raw materials and a solid foundation composed of intuition, compassion, intelligence, and drive. However, we can also be our own worst enemies.

I'll be the first one to admit that sinful behavior can be fun and indulgent, but it can also sabotage your career if you're not careful. As professional women, we commit *Deadly Sins* every day without even knowing it—and, without realizing the damaging consequences.

Here's some good news...despite the description *Deadly Sins*, none of these behaviors represent permanently debilitating or fatal conditions. Unlike personality, which we know forms by the time we celebrate our fifth birthdays, behavior is learned. And, because it is learned, it can be unlearned. Patterns of thinking can be modified. And, with practice and patience, new behaviors and beliefs can pave new paths to success.

The best analogy (simplistic yet effective) I can think of is an impeccably dressed woman: head to toe, she is stunning. She's having a great hair day, her suit looks custom-made, and her stilettos just walked off a Paris runway. She has about 90% of what she needs to put together a complete outfit. Then, she achieves the final 10% when she adds the perfect accessories. The accessories may be small—a few bracelets, earrings, or a necklace—but the impact is enormous and takes the outfit to a whole new level. Impeccable. Extraordinary. Memorable. Complete.

That's exactly the mission of this book: *to deliver the final accessories (I like to call them "successories") that take your career to a new level of success.* It's a roadmap for how to avoid potential potholes and pitfalls, and a guide to demonstrate how small changes can lead to big results. Basically, you have nearly everything you need today. You're 90% of the way there, but for some reason you're struggling to get ahead. Now it's time to think about what changes, tweaks, and modifications you can make that will have an enormous impact on your career. If you're frustrated, disappointed, and falling short of your full potential, then it's time...

It's time to pull on those big-girl panties, get real, and *WOMAN UP!* It's time to hold up the mirror and remove the blinders. It's time to slip on those steel-heeled stilettos (metaphorically speaking) and walk a little taller, strut a little stronger, and show the world who you really are.

Women are a force to be reckoned with, and I intend to celebrate their power, highlight their inner warrior, and encourage them to bring their fabulousness to the workplace—in a purposeful, proactive, and positive way. WOMAN UP! is a recognition that women already possess incredible strength, it's a rallying cry for women to inspire other women, and it's a call to action for all of us.

"I love to see a young girl go out and grab the world by the lapels. Life's a bitch. You've got to go out and kick ass."
—Maya Angelou

If you're just starting out in your career, this is the advice you need. And if you're a seasoned professional, this is the advice you always wished you had. WOMAN UP! is that not-so-gentle reminder for all of us to show up at work as the strong, capable, and amazing women we were born to be.

My goal is to empower women to dig deep and to take control. If we created the behaviors, then we have the power to change them. We have the ability to unlearn harmful behaviors and adopt new, successful ones. We can take the bull by the horns and not wait for times or circumstances to change. We can step up, take action, and do the work to become the best we can be. We can pull on those big-girl panties, find the strength, and gain the confidence to WOMAN UP!

Mirror, Mirror on the Wall

If you are tired of falling short and not achieving your career goals, then it's time to look in the mirror. Just as the magic mirror on the Evil Queen's wall cannot lie, when we look deeply at ourselves in our own mirrors, we uncover the truth. It's time to examine what's getting in your way and make a change. Change is a choice. Attach action to choice and you have movement. And movement is a prerequisite for change.

"Within you is the power to do anything...with confidence and inspiration, you unlock the possibilities."

—Kristin Gibbs

True, we don't always see ourselves the way others see us. We're not always aware of how we're perceived. Sometimes we don't realize that saying yes to everything hurts our careers, or that it's ok for someone not to like us, or that our body language can send the wrong message. Sometimes we limit ourselves without even knowing it.

Women are completely capable of replacing self-destructive thoughts and behaviors with successful strategies. Women are fearless warriors, leaders, and advocates for their children, elderly parents, best friends, and favorite charities. They have herculean inner strength and laser focus when it comes to defending their families or championing a cause, but somehow women don't always exhibit that same ferocity and self-confidence in the workplace.

As we take this journey of self-discovery and positive change together, I will share my own guilty confessions and highlight all the sins (well, maybe not ALL the sins!) I have committed. I truly wish I had this information, advice, and wisdom when I started out in my career. I wish someone could have helped me diagnose my self-limiting behavior and toxic thinking. It would have saved me a lot of heartache and a lot of mistakes.

So, here's my first confession. Initially, I intended to write this book to help women help themselves, but I discovered along the way that I also needed to relearn some valuable lessons and practice more of what I preach. As I tell my own story you will see that I have been guilty of the same self-sabotaging behaviors. Grab a cup of tea (or a glass of wine), put your feet up, and prepare to *WOMAN UP!*

My Story—The Empty Desk

Based on more than 20 years of demonstrated results, my clients, colleagues, friends, family, and community consider me a successful career coach. However, I have also struggled painfully with self-destructive thoughts and behaviors, even while writing this book. (*Who am I to write a book? Even if I do write it, it'll never be good enough. There must be at least a million other, much more qualified people who could do a much better job. What if no one reads it? What if people read it and they hate it?*) I battled a destructive internal dialogue every time I attempted to sit down at my computer to start writing. Sound familiar?

I graduated from the University of Michigan (Go Blue!) in 1989 and, like a lot of other fresh grads, I had absolutely no idea what I wanted to do with my life. I majored in Political Science because I really liked the topics and the teachers. I found the classes thought-provoking and interesting and entertained the idea of going to law school. My family always told me I was gifted at arguing a point and would never back down (my husband and kids certainly agree!). In retrospect, this was probably a euphemism for an angry, argumentative teenager but it sounded like a trial lawyer's core competency to me.

At the time, I wasn't completely sold on the idea of law school and thought I needed some practical work experience first. The problem was that I couldn't find any practical work experience...rather, no one would hire me.

To me, it seemed that jobs were being handed out like Halloween candy. My boyfriend (later my husband) and all my friends didn't seem to have any trouble starting their careers; then there was me. Perhaps there was a secret password or handshake I was supposed to know that everyone else knew. It felt like everyone else received an invitation to the biggest party of the year, except for me.

I thought that there must be something seriously wrong with me. I must be broken in some major way. The hiring managers must have taken one look at me and detected a catastrophic quality that certainly would have caused the demise of their entire organization if they mistakenly made me an offer. As a result, no one invited me to the party.

Time for "Plan B". If I wasn't meant to be gainfully employed, perhaps it was time to revisit those law school applications. After all, I was getting more and more defensive and argumentative by the minute...ideal qualities for a litigator. I studied diligently for the LSATs and did fairly well, though not exceptional, and applied to two law schools in Chicago. As I waited for a response, I mustered up as much confidence as I could. Of course, I thought, I would receive at least one acceptance and then I would begin my new life as a law student.

Instead, I received two rejection letters. Apparently, the wise and omniscient admissions officers must have read something in my essays that told them I was not law school material.

After many tears, hours of introspection, and endless pep talks from family and friends, I decided to try again. Perhaps my boyfriend was right...they had clearly made a mistake and would see the error of their ways the second time around. Evidently, they didn't make a mistake. The second time around, I received two more rejection letters. It was an extremely low point in my life. I felt horrible about myself, my abilities, and my prospects of ever having a fulfilling career.

Even though I was overflowing with self-doubt and sinking deeper into depression, I had bills to pay. It was time to reactivate what I already knew would be yet another unsuccessful job search. This time, I miraculously managed to secure several interviews, but still no offers. As stubborn and independent and unwilling as I was to let anyone help me (again, great lawyer qualities), my grandparents insisted on putting an end to my misery and called their friend, the executive director of the Chicago Bar Association...and he gave me a job.

> *"You may be disappointed if you fail, but you are doomed if you don't try."*
>
> **—Beverly Sills**

Today that initiative would be called "networking", but in my case in the early '90s, it was sheer nepotism. And I was happy to have it.

I can't tell you the title of the position because it didn't have one. What did it have?

An empty desk.

Each day, I literally sat outside the executive director's office in the hallway at an empty desk. But, it didn't matter. I finally had a job. I had a place to go every day and got to ride the "El" downtown with all the other professional commuters. I finally had a purpose and a destination, and, most importantly, my painful, judgment-filled job search was finally over.

I was filled with such a sense of relief I didn't care that I was spending eight hours a day sitting by myself at an empty desk in the hallway. There wasn't a pen, a piece of paper, or a paperclip in sight. It really was just an empty, wooden desk. The previous occupant had carved a heart in the upper right-hand corner. The drawers were equally as empty, except for the one that was permanently locked, its key as lost as the forlorn desk.

My chair wasn't much better and looked like it was recovered (or perhaps liberated) from an old storage room. Not only was the chair old, it was also broken. I was perpetually reclining or leaning awkwardly to the side, tempting gravity daily. There may have been an office pool betting on when I would crash to the floor.

I had a no-name job, a battered desk, and a broken-down chair, and I believed that was what I deserved. My only value at that time was to take up space in the hallway. To make matters worse, I also felt an exorbitant amount of pressure to not be a complete embarrassment to my grandparents. It was one thing to let myself down, but letting my grandparents down would have been downright devastating.

My support system worked tirelessly to fill me with confidence, compliments, and praise and I slowly started to believe that perhaps I had more to offer than merely taking up space at an empty desk. What I didn't realize at the time was that the empty desk wasn't just an empty desk...it was really an *opportunity* in disguise.

The one advantage of sitting at an empty desk all day without a job description or any kind of professional responsibilities was that I had plenty of time to think. And one day I finally thought about the empty desk differently. It was a clean slate, it was potential, and it was the beginning of bigger and better things. It was whatever I wanted it to be.

"The ladder of success is best climbed by stepping on the rungs of opportunity."

—Ayn Rand

It was amazing...once I changed my perspective about the empty desk, everything else changed. The reality was that I was "in". The tough part was over and I could transform this empty, magical desk into my dream job. And that's exactly what happened. It didn't happen overnight, but it was the start of the journey.

I started by introducing myself to all the various departments within the Chicago Bar Association, offering my services and a helping hand wherever I could. I was developing relationships and paying close attention to which areas and projects piqued my interest, where my talents were best suited, and where I felt I was a good match. I was shopping, trying on as many different roles and responsibilities as I could before I found the best fit. I was still hesitant and unsure of myself, but I stayed committed to my new plan of action.

It didn't take long before an advertising sales representative position became available in the Publications Department. It was the opportunity I was waiting for, but I needed to dig deep and to find the courage to go for it. I had no idea how to sell advertising space, but decided to adopt a "fake it 'til you make it" type of attitude and apply. I knew the guys in the department and had already developed great relationships with them. In fact, my formal interview process consisted of only one question: "What's your favorite radio station?" I know that may sound silly, but my new co-worker, Dave, and I would be sharing an office the size of a single cubicle, so our musical compatibility was extremely important.

"Find the thing that ignites your passion, engages your mind, and dare to lead."

—Christiane Amanpour

The best thing about working at an empty desk is that it doesn't take long to pack. The following Monday, Dave and I became office-mates and I started learning how to sell advertising space for the monthly magazine. I quickly understood the strategies behind sales and marketing, but I also understood that the position was not my passion. I couldn't have cared less whether a client bought a quarter or half-page advertisement... not the best mindset to be a successful sales rep.

In my heart, I knew I was born to do something that had greater significance and made more of a positive impact on peoples' lives. But what?

Same S***, Different City

I met my husband, Adam Cohen, at the University of Michigan, and he grew up in Boulder, Colorado. We graduated from college in 1989, moved to Chicago, got married in 1992, and then packed up the U-Haul and moved to Denver in 1993.

It wasn't easy, but I left my entire family, all my friends, and my first professional job to start a new life in Colorado. I fell in love with the landscape and lifestyle and we decided to build a life in the Mile High City. While the weather was a lot better, unfortunately, my job search skills remained subpar. All of my old demons were just lurking in the background, biding their time to resurface and ruin my new life.

My husband had worked for a big engineering company in Chicago and its Houston-based subsidiary was relocating its headquarters to Denver several months after we moved. Seamlessly, Adam secured a new position with the subsidiary and spent much of the next three-and-a-half months in Houston. I had a few friends and a devoted father-in-law for support during that time, and my goal was to find a job before Adam returned to Denver. But what job? How? Where?

I was now living in a new city, knew very few people, and my grandparents couldn't just make a phone call to get me a job. I was lost, literally and figuratively. I had no idea what to do or how to get there, and unless an interviewer's only question was about my taste in music, I was pretty sure I was ill-equipped to find a new job. Needless-to-say, I did not achieve my goal of finding a job before Adam and his new company moved to Denver, which only compounded the already overwhelming feeling of failure.

Adam tried desperately to be optimistic and supportive. He resisted the urge to "fix" me and to solve my spiraling crisis situation. I was determined to solve this problem on my own and not be the only 25-year-old without a job. At his company's holiday party, he did, however, introduce me to one of his new co-workers who happened to be dating a national sales recruiter, Thomas Peay.

I learned from Thomas that a recruiter's job is to help people find a job. This was the brilliant solution I had been waiting for and the help I was willing to accept. I met with

Thomas immediately and he quickly scheduled a few interviews for sales positions with several of his clients. After all, I did have two-and-a-half years of (mediocre) advertising sales experience, and there seemed to be plenty of opportunities given that the unemployment rate was only around 4% at the time. It was a formula for success, but my failure rate stayed the same. No offers.

> *"The trouble is, if you don't risk anything, you risk more."*
> **—Erica Jong**

Opportunity Knocks

There were no more tears left. Every ounce of self-confidence that I had was completely gone. There was nowhere to go except back to Thomas' office to try again. I don't know if it was because I'd finally hit rock bottom or because I needed to exhaust my last, tiny drop of courage before giving up, but I walked into his office that day and saw something familiar, something meaningful.

I saw an empty desk!

Most people would have looked right through the empty desk and moved on, but not me. Empty desks and I already had a history. I didn't see an empty desk, I saw an opportunity...I saw potential...I saw my future.

Somehow I summoned that last, miniscule drop of courage like a bucket straining at the end of its rope for water in the deepest well. I choked out the words and said to Thomas,

"You have an empty desk, why not give me a chance?" My heart was pounding and my body was braced for yet another rejection. *Why would he say yes after all his clients said no?* He sat for a moment, smiled, and then asked, "What's your favorite radio station?" Little did Thomas know that was my all-time favorite, and most successful, interviewing question! I answered, "KBCO," and he said, "Let's give it a try and see what happens."

I'd like to think that Thomas gave me a chance because he saw great potential...that he saw something in me that I couldn't see in myself. In his infinite wisdom, he knew I was the right person for the job. But, at the time, I really think he just felt sorry for me and didn't have the heart to say no. Whether it was an insightful business decision or an act of charity, Thomas' generosity and compassion changed my life.

I always say that I wasn't born a career coach, but I was born to BE a career coach. And, it all started with an empty desk and someone believing in me.

"Find out who you are and do it on purpose."

—Dolly Parton

It was 1993, and Thomas and I worked together in the same office, listening to the same music, for five years. He was a highly experienced and successful recruiter and taught me everything he knew about the business. I was immediately attracted to the idea of helping other lost souls, like me, find meaningful and exciting job opportunities. I started working the phones, dialing up business.

Quickly, I remembered the part I most disliked about sales: cold-calling. I didn't like hearing "no" all day. It made me physically sick. I procrastinated endlessly and dreaded dialing the phone. But Thomas was a natural. He loved cold-calling and chatting with current and prospective clients. He could talk his way through any obstacles to get to the hiring manager.

In an effort to be more efficient with our resources (and to get out of cold-calling), I started focusing more attention on finding and preparing our candidates. I spent my time reformatting résumés, conducting interview preparation workshops, and coaching our candidates through the process. It didn't take long before we had a successful division of labor and I had finally found my passion. I was really good at this!

In 1995, I had my first child, Zachary, and I brought him to the office every day. I set up a pack-n-play and made sure to have plenty of interactive toys on hand. Thomas didn't have any kids at the time, but he really bonded with Zachary. After interviewing candidates in a separate office, I would come back to find Zachary sitting on Thomas' lap while he was on the phone. It was an ideal work situation until Zachary got too active to entertain at work and Thomas wanted to fulfill his dream of living in the mountains.

In 1998, my daughter Rachel and my business, Cohen Career Consulting, were born. I definitely don't recommend giving birth to a new business and a new baby at the same time, but that's what happened. I had plenty of clients and a stream of referrals from my days as a recruiter and I tried to manage the work/life balance as best I could. It was slow-going and my greatest challenge was adjusting my professional expectations with my growing personal responsibilities, all while suffering from complete sleep deprivation.

In order to stay sane, I shifted my short-term goals into longer-term dreams and focused on building a business and a brand that could grow as the needs of my family changed. As much as I loved the idea of being a stay-at-home mom, I also knew that I needed professional fulfillment and a whole lot of patience, because it would require considerable time and careful planning to achieve success.

"The future belongs to those who believe in the beauty of their dreams."

—Eleanor Roosevelt

Somehow I managed to blend my personal and professional lives. It didn't always feel balanced, but it always felt right. My children have always been my number one priority and being their mom, my highest reward. Eventually my business grew as my children grew, and I wouldn't have done it any other way. Zachary and Rachel will always be my greatest—but not my only—success.

An Overnight Success...20 Years in the Making

Twenty years later, I have found much of the success and professional fulfillment I craved. I have a nearly 100% success rate in helping clients achieve their goals; I am described as an inspiring and motivating public speaker; I have worked with hundreds of clients at major crossroads in their careers; I have helped men and women, young and old(er), in every industry imaginable. My dream was becoming a reality.

Careers are a critical part of our lives, but very few people receive any formal education, training, or preparation about how to successfully navigate the treacherous waters of finding a new job, changing careers, building a professional brand, negotiating a higher salary, playing office politics, or making a big move up the corporate ladder. This is where I come in.

As you read further and join me on the journey of recognizing your own sinful behaviors and learn how to turn them into strengths, I want you to know that I, too, am guilty of committing each of the *Deadly Sins* many times over. I have opted out of opportunities because I didn't think I had enough experience or expertise. I have put the needs of colleagues ahead of my own because I wanted to be nice. I have said yes to clients when I knew I should have said no. And I have definitely downplayed and diminished my professional value, given far too many services away for free, and undercharged clients for years.

"I am not afraid...I was born to do this."

—Joan of Arc

But, I have faced my fears, insecurities, and harmful behaviors and transformed two empty desks into a fulfilling, long-term career. Sometimes the right opportunities don't show up exactly as you envisioned. Sometimes it's about taking control and creating the career of your dreams. Sometimes you need to pull on those big-girl panties and *WOMAN UP!* And if I can do it, you can do it.

Don't let the *Deadly Sins* sabotage your success.

Your empty desk awaits. Will you look at it with disdain and despair, or sit down, get to work, and forge a pathway to success? Will you *WOMAN UP*!?

In the 20 years I have been coaching professional women, not one of them has ever sat down and said her number one goal was to sabotage her career, her earning potential, or her ability to get ahead. Usually, the goal is the exact opposite. Yet, the *7 Deadly Sins* still creep in, derail success, and destroy careers. Why?

I have identified four main reasons we commit the *7 Deadly Sins* and sabotage our careers. These reasons manifest themselves in the internal dialogue we can't quiet and the excuses to which we give voice that keep us from reaching our full professional potential.

4 Reasons Why Women Sabotage Their Careers

1. I'm a Failure

Some women have experienced failure in the past and therefore start identifying themselves as a "failure". They describe past or current conditions that prove they are a failure. Then, they actually create situations that corroborate their failure belief over and over. For example, they'll apply for a position they know they'll never get, or pursue a certification without studying for the test, just to prove they're a failure.

They tell themselves and others, "*See, I told you I was a failure and was never going to amount to much.*" It's the victim mentality and a self-fulfilling prophecy. It becomes a very uncomfortable comfort zone, but something that feels familiar. And, as the old saying goes, familiarity breeds content.

2. I'm a Fraud

Some women feel that previous accomplishments, acknowledgements, and accolades somehow were a fluke and not fully deserved. Women lack ownership of their successes and the confidence that they can keep the winning streak alive. They think, "*If people really knew the truth, they'd know I have no idea what I'm doing. I'm an imposter.*" This is not simple modesty; it's an expression of self-doubt characterizing a scarcity of self-belief.

"*Our deepest fear is not that we are inadequate. Our deepest fear is that we are powerful beyond measure. It is our light, not our darkness, that frightens us. We ask ourselves, who am I to be brilliant, gorgeous, talented and fabulous? Actually, who are you not to be?*"

—Marianne Williamson

Women feel tremendous anxiety and stress while worrying that the truth will eventually come out: that they're a fraud who doesn't really know what they're talking about. They fear that somehow, someone will look behind the green curtain and realize that the "Great and Powerful Oz" is nothing more than a weak, old man with a microphone. That's why they self-sabotage and avoid situations where their weaknesses or vulnerabilities could potentially be exposed.

3. I'm Afraid

Some women have a colossal fear of failure and, at the same time, a debilitating fear of success. The "what ifs" become paralyzing. *"What if I fail? I'll be so embarrassed, I'll have to run off and hide from all the shame I have caused myself and others. The disappointment will be so overwhelming I may never get out of bed. I'll lose everything and end up homeless."*

"This is how women self-sabotage and self-destruct. Unless we have constant witness to our hard work, we are convinced we pull off every day of our lives through smoke and mirrors."

—Sarah Ban Breathnach

Amazingly, this represents a real fear for women. According to a poll by Allianz Life Insurance Company of North America, "49% fear becoming a bag lady—a homeless woman who wanders the streets of a city lugging her meager belongings in a shopping bag. Almost half of all women who responded say they 'often' or 'sometimes' fear losing all their money and becoming homeless."

The flipside is equally as daunting. "*What if I succeed? Then the expectations will be greater, a higher goal will need to be set, my whole life will change, I'll be more successful than my partner and that will disrupt the balance of power in our relationship, or there will be a new, bright light shining on my performance and I won't be able to fly under the radar. I don't know how to handle success.*"

The basis of these fears is really the fear of the unknown. What if it works out? What if it doesn't work out? What will people think of me? What will I do next? You won't need to face the unknown if you don't approach it. There is safety and security in not trying, and taking a risk requires surrendering control. And, if there is one thing women love more than almost anything, it is control.

4. I'm Unworthy

Low self-esteem and feelings of unworthiness run rampant among my female clients. They don't think they're smart enough, accomplished enough, or successful enough to be worthy of advancement, recognition, or more money.

According to Dr. Ilona Jerabek, president of PsychTests, "When a person suffers from low self-esteem, it acts like a virus, spreading and infecting the individual's thought patterns, feelings, and behaviors. Your self-doubt results in decisions that reflect your lack of faith in yourself, like not going for that job, not asking that person out, or not asserting yourself when you should."

"Having a low opinion of yourself is not 'modesty.' It's self-destruction. Holding your uniqueness in high-regard is not 'egotism.' It's a necessary precondition to happiness and success."

—Bobbe Sommer

It's especially prevalent for women in the job-search process (which we will discuss later), because the process is filled with judgment, competition, and vulnerability. Women will intentionally self-sabotage and take themselves out of the process prematurely because they lack the confidence and self-worth needed to withstand the scrutiny and to go the distance.

A Prison of Our Own Creation

Here's a very interesting truth: many women are fully aware of "why" they hold themselves back. They know they feel like a failure, have an intense fear of success or failure, or suffer from chronic low self-esteem. What few women realize is "how" they sabotage themselves and potentially kill their careers.

For instance...they're too kind, too competent, too perfect, too needy, too revealing, too confused, or too willing to downplay their accomplishments. They don't have enough perspective to see themselves accurately and to recognize certain behaviors that sabotage their success.

It's true that none of us see ourselves exactly as others see us, and that's why it's so helpful to have an outside, objective perspective. There is great value in a professional career coach, mentor, friend, partner, family member, or spouse holding up the mirror so we can see ourselves clearly—as long as we are ready and willing to accept the feedback.

Because so many of my coaching sessions focus on "how" my female clients sabotage their careers, each chapter highlights one of the *7 Deadly Sins* women commit, shares real-life stories to illustrate the sins and their salvation, reveals my own guilty confessions, and provides career coaching solutions so you can achieve the professional success you deserve.

"Don't be afraid of your own strength."

—Diane Von Furstenberg

Remember the good news? These *Deadly Sins* are only deadly if you allow them to be. They are universal life lessons that many women have experienced, learned from, and triumphed over. Yes, you can write the fairy tale ending to your story—not by waiting for Prince Charming to slip a glass slipper on your foot, but by standing up, sliding into those steel-heeled stilettos, and taking confident strides forward. It's up to you to *WOMAN UP!*

"If your number one goal is to make sure that everyone likes and approves of you, then you risk sacrificing your uniqueness, and, therefore, your excellence."

—Unknown

B eing kind is a virtue, but is being too kind a detriment? It's a fine line, but one that's easily crossed by many working women.

We all know someone who could be described as the "nicest girl in the world". She's the best friend, the sister, the mother that always goes the extra mile and doesn't seem to have the word "no" in her vocabulary. She never says an unkind word and is extremely polite...and would be absolutely devastated if she thought someone didn't like her.

These qualities may serve you well in a social setting, but they can actually derail your career if you're not careful. You don't need to be unkind in order to further your agenda, but being too kind can sabotage your success and the goals you're trying to achieve. It's a conundrum.

"You Like Me, Right Now, You Like Me!" —*Sally Field*

Whether we're working or winning an Oscar, our innate desire to be liked can easily spiral out of control. These feelings may start in grade school, but they continue into adulthood and into the workplace. In school, girls are kind to avoid being called a "mean girl". In the workplace, women are kind to avoid being called a "bitch".

"When a man gives his opinion, he's a man. When a woman gives her opinion, she's a bitch."

—Bette Davis

The labels are different, but the motivation is the same. Most women want to be liked above all else, and because the need to be liked is so strong, women will avoid certain situations and opt out of opportunities where they might be perceived poorly. As a result, self-sabotaging behaviors ensue—

avoiding an unsatisfactory performance review, suppressing an opposing opinion at a board meeting, or deciding not to negotiate a higher salary because someone might not like you.

Tricia and the Lunch Ladies

My client, Tricia, was a well-respected and well-liked director at a non-profit organization. It was a prominent position worthy of a prominent seating position at the annual luncheon. Before Tricia's promotion to director, the women who organized the event would routinely seat her in the back of the room far away from the leadership team and distinguished guests.

Tricia assumed that her new position would also include a new seating assignment at the event. When she realized that, once again, she was relegated to the back of the room she was offended, insulted, and confused about what to do next.

If she confronted the other women and asked them to rearrange the seating chart, would they think she was acting like an entitled diva? Would they think she had an inflated ego? Was this issue worth the potential conflict and fallout? Would they still be friends? Would they say negative things behind her back?

These were all the questions Tricia was struggling to answer. But the real question was, "Would the other women still like her?" Tricia was a woman in a position of power and successfully exceeded all her goals and objectives. However, she was still paralyzed at the possibility that the other women wouldn't like her or would think badly of her if she pushed the issue and flexed her authoritative muscle.

Tricia's initial reaction was to ignore the situation and do nothing. She decided the issue didn't warrant ruffling anyone's feathers. In other words, she wasn't willing to risk the "bitch" label in order to have a more prominent seat at the luncheon.

Doing nothing and avoiding the conflict altogether is not a successful strategy. Too often, women take the path of least resistance and don't fully realize how that self-sabotaging behavior negatively impacts their career.

There are times to do nothing and there are times to take action. This was a time to take action, and we figured out a way for Tricia to stay true to herself, to ruffle the least amount of feathers, and to achieve the desired results. Tricia also needed validation that she was not making unnecessary demands, acting like an entitled diva, or abusing her new position of power.

"A woman should always be more concerned with standing up for what is right than making sure everyone 'likes' her."
—Dr. Laura Schlessinger

She approached the event planners and said, "I'm not sure if this was an oversight or not, but I think it would be really beneficial to the organization if I sit at the front table in order to develop better relationships with the top donors." Tricia did not accuse the women of intentionally sabotaging her seating position and she didn't "pull rank" and throw her director title in their faces.

Instead, she simply focused on the professional value the new seating arrangement would bring to the organization. The women fully agreed, thanked her for bringing the issue to their attention, and seated her at the appropriate table. Tricia felt empowered and did not allow her sinful need to be liked stop her from achieving her goal.

BFFs...Best Friends Forever

Not only do women want to be liked, but they place an enormous amount of value and importance on their relationships, even at work. I have had too many clients fail to pursue a promotion or opportunity because their friend and co-worker had expressed an interest in that new position.

Karen and Her Act of Kindness

Karen was working for a major telecommunications company in the accounting department along with her friend and co-worker, Jamie. They worked together for years and had become extremely close friends. The manager of the department was promoted and both women were qualified to fill the open position.

A management position was part of Karen's career plan and she had been working diligently to develop her leadership skills. Meanwhile, Jamie, a single mom, had complained to Karen about the need to make more money. Karen felt bad for her friend and made a conscious decision to make the friendship the top priority and not even apply for the manager position. Jamie was quickly promoted to manager and became Karen's boss.

Karen relayed this story to me a year later when she hired me to help her find a new job. She didn't resent the fact that Jamie received the promotion. She resented the fact that she didn't even apply for the job. She regretted not having a conversation with her friend about how important the manager position was to her and that they should both apply...and may the best woman win.

Karen held herself back and sabotaged her own career goals because she felt bad for Jamie's financial situation. She didn't want to risk ruining their friendship by competing for the same position, and thought it would be awkward to be her friend's boss. Karen valued the friendship more than the opportunity. Ultimately, Karen's friend became her boss, her own resentment grew, and she started looking for a management position with other companies.

"Remove those 'I want you to like me' stickers from your forehead and, instead, place them where they truly will do the most good—on your mirror!"

—**Susan Jeffers**

I am not suggesting that women should be loyal and kind-hearted to their friends in their personal lives, and then become cold-hearted and ruthless in the workplace. You need to be true to yourself and operate with authenticity and integrity in both areas. However, it is perfectly appropriate, and highly recommended, to have a professional agenda and to take steps to advance that agenda without sabotaging yourself.

If I had been coaching Karen at the time, I would have encouraged her to approach Jamie and find a way to honor the friendship and to pursue her career goals simultaneously. Instead, Karen did nothing, Jamie got the promotion, and Karen was left looking for another job.

Being too kind might be the right way to navigate personal interactions, but it doesn't always work well in a professional environment. If you allow someone to cut in front of you in line at the movie theater, would you also allow someone to steal your credit at work? If you allow a friend to dominate the conversation at dinner, would you also allow a co-worker to dominate a meeting you're leading? Taking a more passive position in social situations may be the right move, but is it the right move to be as passive in the workplace?

"Never dull your shine for somebody else."

—Tyra Banks

It boils down to choosing your battles. It might not be worth jockeying for position in the movie theater line, but if you continuously allow someone to steal your credit at work, you run the risk of appearing weak and losing credibility. Opportunities that should be yours will pass you by. *WOMAN UP!* Being too nice can have a definitive, negative impact on your career.

The Apology Anchor

Not only can women be too kind, but they also apologize excessively without truly evaluating if they've done anything wrong. Saying sorry too much is an anchor on your upward mobility. The frequent, indiscriminate apologies drag you down and hold you back.

Women are taught to be well-mannered and learn early on that it's not polite to make others feel uncomfortable or to appear (and act) overtly aggressive or combative. We ask for help by saying, "*I'm sorry to bother you, but can you direct me to customer service?*" Someone bumps into us and we say, "*I'm sorry, excuse me.*" We don't hear someone call our name in a crowded room and we say, "*I'm so sorry, I didn't hear you.*" We interject in a meeting by saying, "*I'm sorry, but in my opinion...*" None of these scenarios would be classified as wrongdoings, but women still feel the need to apologize.

Women over-apologize as a way to avoid conflict and to foster harmony and agreement. A quick apology may represent an effective strategy if the goal is to deescalate a situation and keep the peace. Instead of appearing kind, however, over-apologizers run the risk of appearing like passive doormats...easily walked all over and taken advantage of by others.

Contrary to popular belief, men also apologize in the workplace, but only when they've analyzed the situation and truly believe they've done something wrong. For women, an apology surfaces as an impulsive reaction, a polite response to a situation she wishes to avoid or to smooth over.

According to one study that appeared in *Psychology Science* in 2010, "participants reported in daily diaries all offenses they committed or experienced and whether an apology had been offered. Women reported offering more apologies than men, but they also reported committing more offenses. There was no gender difference in the proportion of offenses that prompted apologies. This finding suggests that men *apologize less frequently than women because they have a higher threshold for what constitutes offensive behavior.*"

"An apology given to appease one's conscience is self-serving and better left unspoken."

—**Evinda Lepins**

According to this study, men don't find that their own actions and behavior, or those of others, necessitate an apology as frequently. This is good news for women at work—they can act now and ask for forgiveness later (if at all!).

The sinful, overly-polite behavior sends the wrong message in the workplace. Excessive apologizing is perceived as a sign of weakness, a lack of confidence and competence, and an inability to lead and make difficult decisions. The tendency for women to over-apologize at work minimizes their expertise and undermines their authority.

Diane and Her Dilemma

My client, Diane, suffered through the sin of being too kind and over-apologizing. Diane was vice president of operations and the part of her job she dreaded most was conducting performance reviews. She began every review with, "I'm so sorry to have to do this" and then proceeded nervously and timidly to provide the necessary feedback as nicely as she could. Often times, her subordinates felt compelled to make Diane feel better during the review. "That's ok," they would say, "I think the feedback will really help me."

Not only did this behavior reflect poorly on Diane during the reviews, but it caused her subordinates to lose respect for her as a leader after the reviews. And, unfortunately, they often missed critical information and feedback because of Diane's apologetic delivery.

The ability to apologize and to accept responsibility is a noble quality in the right circumstances. Conversely, unconscious and indiscriminate apologizing can damage your career. If women want to achieve greater levels of respect and success, being more selective and discerning about when to say "I'm sorry" is a step in the right direction. *WOMAN UP!* and reserve your apologies for truly offensive behavior and egregious errors.

Turning the Tables

Other women occupy the opposite end of the Kindness Conundrum spectrum—those who believe they need to be "mean girls" in order to get ahead. They operate with a significantly more aggressive, masculine, and domineering style in the workplace. Often, this behavior is a result of feeling insecure and threatened by other successful women (and men). However, unlike their counterparts, these women act as if they don't care if they're liked or not. They view their abrasive and "unlady-like" behavior as a strength, not a weakness, and maintain their positions of power through fear and intimidation.

Not only do these qualities conjure up bad "mean girl" memories for many of us, but they come across as anti-woman and off-putting. As women have advanced in the corporate arena and started penetrating the so-called "old boys" network, a conscious or subconscious mindset surfaced; in order to be accepted and respected, women thought they needed to act like men, dress like men, and reject feminine characteristics. Not true, as this next true tale demonstrates.

Ann and Her Axe

My client, Ann, worked in local government, a traditionally male-dominated industry. She had a very direct and abrasive communication style and lacked the subtle nuances that women use when navigating a conversation. She came across as aggressive, cold, and combative, and her biggest problem was that she couldn't retain any female employees. Ann's department had the highest turnover rate and her boss was pressuring her to hire and retain more women.

In my first 5 minutes with Ann, I knew exactly why the turnover rate was so high among the female employees. Ann was not a "girl's girl". She admitted she was harder on the women in the department because "they needed to develop a thicker skin if they wanted to work in government".

Granted, Ann believed she was doing her female employees a favor, but the plan completely backfired. I worked with Ann to help her realize that softening her approach was not a sign of weakness, but a sign of strength and better leadership. As she modified her behaviors, her team environment and retention rate improved.

Fortunately, over the years I have encountered fewer and fewer "mean girls", but I still work with plenty of women struggling with the Kindness Conundrum. There is a fine line between being kind and being *too* kind. If you're not achieving the professional goals you have set for yourself and you've identified a destructive pattern of "kind" behavior, it may be time to *WOMAN UP!* and replace your wishbone with a backbone.

🔪 Guilty Confession 🔪

I actually committed the full range of "kindness" sins in a single scenario. I started off too kind, apologized excessively, and then turned into a mean girl from the depths of hell. It was a complete disaster that turned into an important life lesson.

I was hired to facilitate a 5-day transition workshop for a *Fortune 500* telecommunications company. The terms of the contract were pretty straightforward and I was really excited to do what I do best—deliver useful career information in an entertaining and action-oriented workshop. The consultant who hired me to help his client was a really nice guy and we had a successful working relationship in the past.

On the first day, Monday, it became obvious that there was a major miscommunication snafu between the host company and the workshop participants. Although the participants were supposed to be divided evenly over the 5 days, instead, everyone showed up on the first day. Being the "nice girl", I didn't want this logistical disaster to reflect poorly on my consultant friend, so I put forth great effort to make the best of the situation. I conducted additional workshops and scheduled private one-on-one consultations throughout the remainder of the week. Despite all the challenges, the participants enjoyed a highly productive experience and raved about the content and results they achieved. Everyone was happy.

I submitted my invoice and awaited the final payment. I waited the appropriate 30 days and then I contacted my friend and said, *"I'm so sorry to bother you, but do you have any idea when I'll receive the final payment?"*

Why in the world was I apologizing? He was late with the payment, yet I was apologizing. That's crazy. What's even crazier is that my apologizing went on for another 60 days as my invoice went unpaid. Clearly that approach wasn't working.

At this point, I passed right by the freeway entrance marked "mean girl" and accelerated into the "insane mafiosa" express lane. I was ready to break knee-caps as if I were collecting on a bad debt. I started demanding my payment and making all kinds of ridiculous statements such as, *"If I was a man, you wouldn't even think about lying to me that the check is in the mail!"* As if that weren't bad enough, I even made some idle threats that I'm too embarrassed to recall. I believe I was trying to channel my inner Cruella de Vil.

I didn't feel good about losing control and going to that uber-aggressive extreme to get results. However, I felt that I had been exceptionally kind and accommodating so my friend could be successful in the eyes of his client. Then the pendulum swung so far the other way and, as my resentment built up, so did my mean-girl antics. Neither of us felt good about the interaction and it was a major life lesson to me as a woman and business owner. It's just like Goldilocks...you don't want to be too nice or too mean. You want to find that happy medium and be "juuuuuuust right".

⚞ Success Solutions ⚟

Finding the happy medium is not always easy and may require a little trial and error before you find the right balance. Assess the situation and your options, seek feedback if necessary, and then respond accordingly. The goal is self-awareness and recognizing if either of those ends of the spectrum are interfering with your success, and then making the necessary adjustments.

If there is a Goldilocks in your office, a woman who successfully straddles that line between too nice and too mean, then she is one to watch. Imitation is the greatest form of flattery. Pay close attention and model your behavior after someone who has already found the right balance.

We are all works-in-progress and one thing we can certainly work on is being a little more selective about when to say, "I'm sorry." It's time to stop indiscriminately apologizing for things we shouldn't feel sorry about in the first place. It only diminishes our power and lessens the respect we rightfully deserve. Now, *WOMAN UP!*, raise your right hand, and swear that you will no longer apologize unnecessarily for the following things...

10 Things For Which You May *NEVER* Apologize

1. **Your Ambition.** Why is it acceptable for men to set their sights on the C-suite or corner office, but not for women? Don't apologize for your drive and determination. If you're goal-oriented and work hard for promotions, awards, and recognitions, then simply say, "Thank you" not "I'm sorry".

2. **Your Balance.** Never apologize for seeking balance. If spending quality time with your family or following an exercise routine is important to you, find a way to make it work. Proudly put those things at the top of your own priority list. Men make time to play golf and to coach their kids' soccer games, so why shouldn't women? A well-balanced woman is a more successful woman.

3. **Your Brilliance.** Being the smartest girl in class is an asset, not a detriment. Don't apologize if other people didn't do their homework. Dumbing yourself down was not an

attractive quality in the classroom and it's not an attractive quality in the boardroom. Embrace the beauty of your brilliance, and don't apologize for it.

4. **Your Expertise.** Being a subject matter expert or leader in your industry doesn't happen by accident and it doesn't happen overnight. It takes years of hard work and dedication to build a reputation as an expert. Don't minimize your significance so others can feel important. Own your expertise...you earned it.

5. **Your Failures.** If you're not failing, then you're not trying hard enough. Instead of apologizing for a misstep, a mistake, or a complete blunder, embrace the fact that you took a risk. Make the necessary changes and adjustments—just don't make an apology.

6. **Your Individuality.** Everyone likes to "fit in" to a certain extent, but what if you march to the beat of a different drum? If you think outside of the box, if your career path is more crooked than straight, then embrace and celebrate your individuality and don't apologize for it.

7. **Your Intuition.** As women, we are fortunate to possess the gift of intuition. That little voice and gut feeling are there for a reason. Instead of ignoring the signs and apologizing for a "feeling", trust yourself and listen to your intuition.

8. **Your Personality.** Blending into the background and being invisible is not always an option. If you have a big, boisterous personality, don't apologize for it...just be aware of the situation. Being the life of the party may be who you are, but it's not always your party. Be sensitive, not apologetic.

9. **Your Success.** Success is a goal, not a gift. No one gives it to you, you earn it. You work hard and sacrifice for success and should never diminish it by apologizing. No man would ever say, "I'm sorry I'm the CEO," so why should you? Be proud of your accomplishments.

10. **Your Value.** Whether you're negotiating a base salary, seeking a raise, or establishing your hourly fee, apologizing for rightfully earning money for your valuable products, services, and expertise is no longer acceptable. Remove "I'm sorry, but I charge $250 an hour" from your vocabulary. Negotiate with confidence. Super-successful women not only don't apologize for how much money they make, they know they're worth every penny.

◢ WOMAN UP! Reflections ◣

1. Have you committed the "Kindness Conundrum" sin? Give an example.

   _____

   _____

   _____

   _____

   _____

   _____

2. How has it impacted your career?

   _____

   _____

   _____

   _____

   _____

   _____

3. How do you plan to change it?

   _____

   _____

   _____

   _____

   _____

   _____

"If you want something said, ask a man; if you want something done, ask a woman."

—Margaret Thatcher

I t's true...women are doers. But are we doing too much?

We are professionals, mothers, wives, best friends, daughters, mentors, volunteers, and sisters. We are genetically designed and evolutionarily equipped to perform a variety of roles with a variety of responsibilities on a daily basis. Since cavemen (and cavewomen) roamed the earth, men have been the hunters and women have been the gatherers. Evolution and societal roles have hard-wired multi-tasking into our DNA...we can't help ourselves.

This "I can do it all" attitude may have been critical to the survival of early civilization, but as we moved out of the caves and into more complicated lives, this attitude also needs to evolve.

"You can't be all things to all people, so don't even try."
—Rachael Ray

The big question is: *Do you suffer from the Competency Curse?* Just because we CAN do it all, doesn't necessarily mean we SHOULD. Unfortunately, we carry this prehistoric multi-tasking, overly-competent behavior into the workplace. We want to do everything ourselves and be everything to everyone. *WOMAN UP!* and make the tough decisions about what takes priority and what takes a pass. The reality is that being too competent can sabotage your success.

3 Dangers of Being Too Competent

1. Becoming "Jill" of All Trades, Master of None

In today's marketplace, it's all about being an expert. It's not about being average at a hundred different things; it's about being the best at a select few. Highly competent people have the innate ability to accomplish many things, but spreading yourself too thin and not being selective about where you apply your skills can ruin your career.

You want to be known for something specific and to be recognized for a marketable talent. Being associated with a wide variety of unrelated skills and projects is too vague, too confusing, and ultimately forgettable...and if you're forgettable, you're dispensable.

Spend your time becoming the master of something specific and people will remember you, hire you, promote you, reward you, retain you, and celebrate you.

2. Getting Dumped On

When you're highly competent, people often take notice and take advantage of you. When people realize you have the ability to complete a task, meet a deadline, and serve as a resource, you will get a lot of extra assignments dumped on your desk.

It's not that you "can't" complete those assignments, but is that the best use of your time? If you use all your time helping other people and being that "go-to" employee, you won't have time to pursue the opportunities that could take your career to the next level.

It's easy to want to put all of our competencies into action when our egos are triggered. It's hard to say no when your co-worker says, "*I can't do this without you,*" or "*You're the only one who can help me.*" It feels great to be needed, wanted, and appreciated. Just be careful that being "dumped on" is not derailing your own career goals.

3. Lacking Leadership

Powerful and effective leaders are seen as decisive, clear, and focused. They also have the confidence to surround themselves with super-smart people that they can delegate to and then support. True leaders set others up for success.

"There is no sin in delegating. The sin is trying to do it all."
—Deborah Roberts

A highly competent person can easily morph into a control freak and hoard all the responsibilities and information. They think, *"No one else can do it as well, accurately, fast, or efficiently as I can."* Nothing could be further from the truth! If you have leadership aspirations, then the professional development of others and their success needs to top your priority list. You want to provide others with the tools, skills, resources, and opportunities to be successful...not do it all yourself.

Competency is only a curse if you allow it to be. Even though you may "want" to do it all, know that you "can" do it all, doing it all yourself ultimately stifles your growth and kills your career. Align yourself with other competent people and then you can do it all together. If you focus your skills in a particular area, ensure you have time to actively pursue those skills, and then delegate the rest...you'll find that competency is not really a curse, but a blessing.

The Disease to Please

Wanting to be all things to all people is the diagnostic description of the "disease to please". Again, just because we CAN doesn't necessarily mean we SHOULD.

Women multi-task to the point where they are overloaded, overwhelmed, and underappreciated. Spreading yourself too thin in the workplace and assuming an unrealistic amount of additional responsibilities are unfortunate symptoms of the "disease to please". But what's the cause?

> *"Everyone's so timid and afraid to insult anybody, but in the end, it's like we're all trying to please everyone. In the end, we please no one."*
>
> **—Olivia Munn**

Surprisingly, toddlers actually possess the key to success. That's right, that little monster running your life holds the key. Toddlers have the innate ability to say "no"—willingly, freely, and frequently—to almost anything without reservation or hesitation. Unfortunately, that ability diminishes as we age. We say "yes" far too often when we really should be saying "no". It's time to take a lesson from the "terrible twos", and embrace the power of a simple two-letter word.

Jennifer and Her Job-Hopping

My client, Jennifer, definitely suffered from the disease to please and it became painfully obvious as she described her decision-making process in accepting job offers. She could easily be described as a job-hopper, with seven jobs in five years, but that was never part of her master career plan. When I asked her why she accepted so many ill-suited job offers, she simply said, "Well, they said they really needed me and I just couldn't say no."

The seemingly desperate pleas of the hiring managers to join their sales teams made Jennifer feel special, heroic, and exceptionally competent. She loved feeling needed. Obviously, none of the jobs worked out, and Jennifer soon learned that it could also feel good to say "no".

Highly successful people already recognize the power of saying "no", but it's important to examine some of the reasons why women have a natural tendency say "yes".

5 Reasons Why Women Say "Yes"

1. Saying "Yes" Feels Good

Saying "yes" is often an emotional or impulsive response. It's flattering to be asked to lead a project at work, to accept a new job offer, to sit on a board or committee, to attend an event, or to donate your time and expertise to a special cause.

Women perceive the "asking" as a compliment and they like to feel needed. They feel as if they were specifically chosen out of everyone else and it triggers an ego-driven response to agree without considering the consequences, extensive time commitment, additional workload, or unexpected sacrifices.

2. Saying "Yes" Is Easy

Saying "yes" is an effective way to avoid potential conflict. It's the path of least resistance and a quick way to end a conversation. There's no begging or pleading or guilt-tripping. No one ever asks you "why?" after you've said "yes". When a woman says "no", she feels the need to justify her answer with an endless list of explanations and excuses.

"'No' is a complete sentence."

—Anne Lamott

3. Saying "Yes" Doesn't Disappoint

Women don't like to disappoint anyone. The sinking feeling of potentially letting down a boss, co-worker, or a friend in need is strong motivation to say "yes". No one ever gives you a sad face or bursts into tears after you've said "yes". But if you don't think it through, that seemingly simple "yes" can come back to bite you. It's a quick answer to a short-term question, but it may create greater disappointment in the long-run.

4. Saying "Yes" Says You're a Superwoman

We're conditioned to believe we can do it all, but it's really just a myth. If a woman says "no", it's as if she's admitting she's the only woman who can't do it all. It's a "do it all" competition. We compare ourselves to other women who clearly have no trouble running a business, managing a family, volunteering at the school, and training for a triathlon (all in the same day!).

The superwoman-myth equally exists in the workplace, and no woman wants to be perceived as incompetent, incapable, or not smart enough to complete an assignment. The superwoman-myth hinders our ability and willingness to ask for help and support when we need it. True, we can do it all; we just can't do it all, all the time.

5. Saying "Yes" Says You're a Team-Player

Saying "yes" sends a clear message that you're not a selfish employee only concerned with her own goals and workload. It's true that organizations value those "team-player" employees, but women take that to the extreme by saying "yes" to everything. The reality is that saying "yes" to everything does not guarantee job security, and it could actually put you on the fast track to a pink slip if you are not careful.

Sue and Her Sad Outcome

My client, Sue, witnessed many of her co-workers being laid-off when her company downsized, and she was panic-stricken at the thought of losing her job. Her strategy was to say "yes" to absolutely everything, arrive early, stay late, and work on the weekends. Her strategy, however, created a huge, unforeseen problem— her pace was impossible to sustain over a long period of time.

By saying "yes" to everything, Sue established a new, unrealistic set of expectations. She struggled to set boundaries and her boss kept piling on the projects. Sue was miserable, burned out, and eventually forced to look for a new job. By saying "yes" to everything, Sue unwittingly created the outcome she feared the most.

Understanding why women say "yes" is one thing, but it's also important to understand all the additional challenges that are created when we don't say "no"...the unwanted results, unrealistic expectations, and unforeseen consequences.

Saying "yes" when you should say "no" is a formula for over-promising and under-delivering. It's a recipe for disaster and a set-up for failure. Time, energy, and resources are limited, and over-committing your attention to too many responsibilities detracts from your ability to focus on the goals critical to your career. Making unrelated and time-consuming commitments distracts you from what's most important and may prevent you from achieving your own goals.

"When you really want to say no, say no. You can't do everything—or at least not well."

—Anna Quindlen

Saying "yes" to projects that don't properly showcase your skills and talents greatly diminishes your value and position as an expert. You're doing so many things at once and are spread so thin that you're not doing any one thing very well. And, your time is tied up in areas that may not optimize the value you can add. Producing mediocre work for multiple people is actually hurting, not helping, your career.

Indiscriminate multi-tasking also opens the door for co-workers to knowingly or unknowingly take advantage of you. It establishes an expectation that you'll always say "yes" and put the needs of others before your own. It makes you look weak and easily influenced. Being able to appropriately say "yes" or "no" demonstrates confidence, good judgment, and sound decision-making skills.

> "When we don't want to do something we can simply smile and say no. We don't have to explain ourselves, we can just say 'No'."
>
> **—Susan Gregg**

Nancy and Her Note-Taking

My client, Nancy, was a human resources director and was very passionate and knowledgeable about her industry. At one of the first meetings with the senior male executives, someone asked her to take notes, write up the minutes, and send them out to the group. Wanting to be a "team-player", Nancy said "yes" to those administrative duties in the beginning, but then felt continuously frustrated at the assumption that she would do it every time.

Those additional tasks derailed her ability to really participate and to contribute her thoughts during the meeting. It minimized her value as a contributor by positioning her as a "note-taker". It devalued her position and she resented saying "yes" when she should have said "no".

Saying "no" is not always easy, but it does have its benefits.

5 Benefits of Saying "No"

1. Greater Clarity
When you say "no" to extraneous activities and commitments, it provides greater clarity and allows you to discover what's really important. Saying "yes" when you really want to say "no" causes confusion not clarity. Trust that when you say "no", you're really saying "yes" to a greater opportunity that's more aligned with your expertise, goals, and values.

2. Deeper Connections
Developing quality relationships is not only important in our personal lives, it's imperative to the success of our professional lives. Saying "no" to insignificant and unrelated activities allows us to concentrate our efforts on creating meaningful relationships and an effective network with the people that mean the most.

3. More Balance
Success is measured not only in the workplace, but also in life. As much as we would like to compartmentalize our lives and keep our work and home lives separate, we can't. They're all connected. Committing to fewer obligations enables you to relax, to enjoy

more time with family and friends, and to get energized by those activities that bring you joy and feed your soul.

4. Increased Confidence

Saying "no" and setting clear and intentional boundaries increases your confidence in the workplace. It elevates your authority and people take you seriously. Instead of being perceived as easy to manipulate and overly eager to please, people recognize your authority and respect your decision-making. Stand firm, stay confident, and say "no".

5. Faster Success

Saying "no" appropriately and professionally empowers you to expedite and streamline your career path. You can reach your goals faster, more efficiently, and gain greater respect by eliminating, or reducing, the number of irrelevant and time-consuming activities you pursue.

Though we can't throw a tantrum like a toddler, we can fully embrace the power of saying "no" when it's connected to conscious, intentional, and mature decision-making. WOMAN UP! and know when it's right to say "no", be confident in your convictions, and you'll discover the opportunities and actions that truly merit a "yes".

WOMAN UP! *Tips...*
5 Ways to Say "No" with Confidence

1. *That sounds like a great idea, but it doesn't align with my goals at the moment.*

> 2. *I can't commit to this, because I have already filled my pro bono quota for the year.*
> 3. *I'm not the best person for that task; perhaps you should ask Bob?*
> 4. *I wish I could, but as a general rule, I don't work on the weekends.*
> 5. *Thank you for asking, but I need to politely decline.*

At some point in history, asking for help was classified as a weakness and women still perpetuate this myth today. We would rather wake up early, stay up late, run ourselves ragged, or risk failure than ask for help. It is an exhausting, and unrealistic, attempt to keep the Wonder Woman image alive.

The strongest, smartest, and most competent women know how to ask for help and fully embrace and appreciate the help they receive. They identify when they need help and who can help them. Most people truly want to help, especially those close to you, and the greatest gift you can give someone is the opportunity to help you.

As much as we would like to think we're mythical creatures with supernatural powers, capable of managing everything in a single bound, we're not. We're real people with real limitations, and sometimes in need of real help. The Competency Curse will crush your career if you allow it to. Don't sabotage yourself by doing it all yourself…ask for help and finally turn that outdated weakness into your greatest strength.

⚞ Guilty Confession ⚟

I'll admit I'm guilty of this sinful behavior. By definition, my profession as a career coach is all about helping others, but sometimes I don't help myself the way I should. I impulsively say "yes" because I don't want to hurt someone's feelings or because my ego is triggered when someone needs me. Like many of my clients, I instantly regret saying "yes" in certain situations when I know I should have said "no".

Early in my career, I said "yes" to prospective clients I knew were not a good fit for me, my business, or my success rate. It took me a long time to realize that not all clients are good for business. There are those clients that monopolize all your time, drain all your energy, and then quit half way through the process. We all know that some people ask for help, but are not ready to accept the help they need. What they really needed to hear from me was "no". Fortunately, I eventually learned that lesson.

Unfortunately, there are other situations where I didn't learn the lesson nearly as well. For instance, a friend and colleague of mine hosted a local radio show and had parted ways with his co-host. He felt strongly that the show's success was due to having a female co-host and asked me if I was interested in filling that position. He was extremely complimentary about my skills and personality, how I could be an asset to the show, and my natural "radio voice".

I'm embarrassed to admit that emotions clouded my judgment and my natural, sound decision-making skills.

It honestly felt wonderful to be needed and in a position to help a friend. Deep down I knew it wasn't the right venue and audience for my professional message and I didn't have the time to commit to other projects, but I said "yes" anyway.

"We should regret our mistakes and learn from them, but never carry them forward into the future with us."
—Lucy Maud Montgomery

In the end, just like Sue, I created what I feared the most and disappointed my friend when I changed my answer from "yes" to "no". I felt horrible and regretted not having better control over my emotional response. I kicked myself for a long time and swore I would never do that again. I'd be lying if I said I have a perfect track record, but I really do my best to say "no" when I should say "no".

⚑ Success Solutions ⚑

Saying "no" is all about setting boundaries and getting clear about what you really want. If you have trouble uttering that simple two-letter word, then a little help might be just what you need.

To make decision-making easier and more intentional, here is a checklist to help you say "no" when you need to do so.

WOMAN UP! *Tips...*
When to Say "No" Checklist

1. *Do I have the time?*
2. *Does it align with and further my career goals?*
3. *Would I learn any new skills?*
4. *Would I meet influential people to expand my network?*
5. *Would I be successful?*
6. *Would it showcase my greatest strengths and abilities?*
7. *What would I need to give up or sacrifice?*
8. *Would it feed my soul or satisfy a need in my life?*
9. *Would I feel proud to be associated with it?*
10. *Would I be able to leverage the experience for future opportunities?*

Instead of allowing your "disease to please" to completely overshadow your ability to make smart, success-oriented decisions, use this checklist to help make more deliberate and intentional decisions. Cleary, if you answer "no" to all 10 questions on the checklist, then your answer should be "no". At the very least, this will enable you slow down, evaluate the opportunity more objectively, and say "yes" or "no" with more certainty.

Mentors also are helpful when it comes to trying to cure the "disease to please". It's an opportunity to learn from someone else's wisdom and to hear some honest feedback about how your behavior is either helping or hurting your career. Mentors have "been there, done that". They have insight, experience, and perspective that are invaluable in the workplace and in life.

"Mentor: Someone whose hindsight can become your foresight."
—Unknown

If you have identified that indiscriminately saying "yes" when you really should be saying "no" is negatively impacting your career, having a mentor is a wonderfully effective way to modify that behavior. Whether it's a formal mentor who holds you accountable, or an informal mentor who you're trying to emulate, having a role model you respect is an empowering way to learn how to say "no".

It's true...women are doers and we like to do it all. We are super heroes in so many ways. We put on our Wonder Woman gold lasso and bracelets and save the world like a true warrior princess should. But is there an easier way?

Imagine Wonder Woman's learning curve. She didn't have another strong female role model to look up to...she didn't even have a side-kick to help her. She was doing it all by herself.

The question is: would Wonder Woman have been an even greater super hero with a mentor? Statistics say, YES:

- 94% of women owning small businesses who had a mentor say it was "critical" to their success (*Avon's Mentoring Matters* study)

- Training alone increases productivity by 24%; the combination of mentoring and coaching increases productivity by 88% (*American Society for Training & Development*)
- Professionals with mentors earn more, between $5,610 and $22,450 more annually than those who do not (*HR Magazine*)

Mentoring can be a formal or informal relationship. A formal mentoring relationship involves specific goals and objectives and is intended to help facilitate personal and professional growth. It has mutually agreed-upon parameters, guidelines, and timeframes. However, there needs to be a natural, organic connection in order for a formal mentoring relationship to be successful.

"Not until I was asked to be a mentor did I appreciate the responsibility and gift of being one; you are guiding, helping, and inspiring others to fulfill their dreams."
—Graciela Meibar

An informal mentoring relationship looks a little more like selective "hero worship". Who are those people in your industry or profession that you idealize? That you want to emulate? Who is a little further along in her career that you could learn from? Who can you use as a sounding board?

Doing it all by yourself is not always a virtue. The isolated Wonder Woman mentality can hold us back and sabotage our careers. The truth is, we are extremely competent, but we don't have all the answers. We don't always know what to say, where to be, or how to act. There is so much we can learn and improve upon if we simply embrace a mentor.

WOMAN UP! *Tips…*
10 Benefits of Having a Mentor

1. *Identifies potential self-sabotaging behavior.*
2. *Shortens your learning curve.*
3. *Provides critical insight to office politics and personalities.*
4. *Assists you with goal-setting and career decision-making.*
5. *Holds you accountable.*
6. *Is a trusted confidant, answers questions, and provides valuable feedback.*
7. *Opens doors and makes connections.*
8. *Boosts your confidence.*
9. *Serves as a cheerleader and champion.*
10. *Models successful professional behavior and interactions.*

🥿 WOMAN UP! Reflections 🥿

1. Are you guilty of the "Competency Curse"? Give an example.

   _____

   _____

   _____

   _____

   _____

   _____

2. How has it impacted your career?

   _____

   _____

   _____

   _____

   _____

   _____

3. How do you plan to change it?

   _____

   _____

   _____

   _____

   _____

   _____

"Understanding the difference between healthy striving and perfectionism is critical to laying down the shield and picking up your life. Research shows that perfectionism hampers success. In fact, it's often the path to depression, anxiety, addiction, and life paralysis."

—Dr. Brené Brown

W e have all been told that "practice makes perfect"...but does it? Is there really such a thing as perfection? Of course not! It's a myth, a vicious rumor, an elusive goal, a painful trap, and a destructive ideal that we need to acknowledge and put in its proper place.

The pressure for perfection can be overwhelming and damaging to our self-esteem even though we know it's all a façade. We're locked in a Perfectionism Prison. It may not actually have metal bars and a lock and key, but it's powerful enough to keep us trapped inside our own destructive thoughts and behaviors.

Intellectually, we know that perfection doesn't exist, but emotionally we still strive for it. We know that super-models need a glam squad and endless air-brushing to appear flawless in magazines, yet we spend millions of dollars on cosmetic surgery each year to achieve that perfect look. According to the American Society of Plastic Surgeons, 14.6 million cosmetic plastic surgery procedures, including both minimally-invasive and surgical, were performed in the United States in 2012, which is a 5% increase since 2011. Perfection may not be attainable, but we are willing to go under the knife to pursue it.

I'm sure perfectionism existed back in the Stone Age when cavewomen agonized over the cave décor and scoured the plains to find a recipe for the perfect mammoth burgers. In the 1950s, women worried about being the perfect homemaker, the perfect wife, the perfect mother, and the perfect hostess.

> *"The thing that is really hard, and really amazing, is giving up on being perfect and beginning to work on becoming yourself."*
>
> **—Anna Quindlen**

Today, we still aspire to be perfect in all those areas, but we also have added "perfect professional" to the list. Women also can be "perfect" control freaks and that quality can lead to a lot of sinful and self-sabotaging behavior when it comes to career success. Today, we have the Martha Stewart standard to aspire to and perfectionism is more rampant than ever.

Perfectionism is a blessing and a curse all wrapped up in a (perfect) little package. On the one hand, it's admirable and ambitious to set lofty goals for ourselves. That's how we grow and learn. On the other hand, it's a trap that women fall into and inevitably end up feeling disappointed, inadequate, and worthless. There is no such thing as perfection, there is no such thing as perfect timing, and there is no such thing as a perfect career path.

"It's one thing to have drive and discipline, these qualities help you succeed and get noticed by higher-ups," explains Jeff Szymanski, Ph.D., a clinical psychologist and author of *The Perfectionist's Handbook*. "But a perfectionist is so obsessed with being the best she sets unattainable goals for herself—and when she can't achieve them, she feels stress and disappointment that can undermine her performance."

Women adopt an extreme black or white, all or nothing, perfection or failure, type of attitude that produces self-limiting behavior. If the opportunity isn't perfect, if the circumstances aren't perfect, or if the confidence level isn't perfect, women will hold themselves back or take themselves out of the running completely.

A Perfect Opportunity

As a career coach, one of the biggest differences I have found between my male and female clients is the connection between perfection and opportunity. Women want to be the expert first, and then they look for the opportunity. Men find the opportunity first, and then focus on becoming the expert later. The result is that many women miss out on major opportunities. They don't believe they have enough education, work experience, or support from friends and family. Women want to have all their ducks perfectly in a row before they make a move. Men move and then they try to locate their ducks.

WOMAN UP! *Tips…*
You Know You're a Perfectionist When…

1. *You miss deadlines because the project is never good enough to be done.*
2. *You instantly become defensive if someone questions or criticizes you.*
3. *You secretly love it when someone else fails because it makes you look better.*

4.   *You truly believe there are no letters between "A" and "F".*
5.   *You put up a wall so others can't get close enough to see your imperfections.*

For example, when evaluating a job description, women believe they have to have nearly 100% of the requirements in order to apply for the position. Women want a perfect match and a high degree of certainty before moving forward. Otherwise, they will hyper-focus on the one skill they don't have, or don't have enough of, and convince themselves they're completely under-qualified and no hiring manager on earth would ever consider them for an interview. Just for the record, a 100% match with any job description is like walking on the moon...it's possible, but very few people actually experience it.

> *"Perfect is boring. In recognizing our flaws, we find what makes us interesting."*
>
> **—Tyra Banks**

Alice Domar, Ph.D., supported this idea in her *TIME* magazine article, *"Why Do Women Need to Be Perfect?"* She said, "Women are unhappy because, even if 11 out of 12 things are going well, they zero in on the one that isn't, and they get miserable about it."

Men, on the other hand, barely need to match 60% of the job description before rushing to apply. They are more willing to "strike while the iron's hot", and are confident enough in their skills and abilities that they'll be successful in the new role once they get it.

It's not that men don't feel insecure or unsure; it's that they don't allow those negative thoughts to stop them from taking action. Men are much more likely to talk themselves into an opportunity than out of one, while women do the complete opposite. Men will confidently say, "*I can do that*," while women will woefully admit, "*I'm not ready to do that*."

Women become crippled with self-doubt and insecurities to the point where it sabotages their careers. However, a seasoned perfectionist will always provide a perfect excuse as to why she didn't jump at that opportunity.

The reality is that women are low risk-takers and are paralyzed at the thought of looking stupid, silly, or incompetent...of appearing *imperfect*.

WOMAN UP! *Tips...*
A Perfectionist's List of Perfect Excuses

1. *That opportunity really wasn't a good fit.*
2. *Next year I'll have more experience and be more qualified.*
3. *I just need to finish my Master's degree and then I'll be ready.*
4. *I think there's a better job around the corner.*

5. *As soon as my kids are older, I'll go for that promotion.*
6. *I didn't really want all that additional responsibility anyway.*
7. *My family couldn't manage without me if I traveled for work.*
8. *My team needs me and would fall apart if I changed departments.*
9. *I'm sure there's someone else who's much more qualified.*
10. *I've never done that before.*

Vanessa and Her Perfect Job

My client, Vanessa, was a public relations executive. She was bright and successful…and a total perfectionist. After conducting an exhaustive job search, she finally found a seemingly "perfect" position with a "perfect" company. The problem was that once reality set in, and the honeymoon was over, she found herself deeply disappointed and wanting to quit. The new, perfect job did not live up to her expectations and her immediate reaction was to leave. Clearly, the problem was the company and not her unrealistic definition of perfection.

After a few sessions of reviewing and examining her less-than-perfect career history, Vanessa agreed to adjust her expectations and give the new job six months. Vanessa remained in that position and was happy that her perfectionism did not end up sabotaging a great—but not perfect—opportunity.

Not only can the Perfectionism Prison be limiting, but so can the inability to take a risk. The problem is that women can't distinguish a big risk from a little risk, because all risks have the potential to end imperfectly. There is a lack of control and the reward does not seem worth the risk. The way women manage risk is by self-sabotaging, avoiding and declining opportunities that could potentially advance their careers.

"You gain strength, courage and confidence by every experience in which you really stop to look fear in the face. You are able to say to yourself, 'I lived through this horror. I can take the next thing that comes along'...You must do the thing you think you cannot do."

—Eleanor Roosevelt

Vanessa and Her "What Ifs"

At Vanessa's new, not-so-perfect job, she was asked to represent her organization and deliver the keynote speech at a national conference. She was a polished and articulate professional with years of public relations experience, but had never spoken to an audience larger than a conference room, and she seriously considered handing that golden opportunity off to a co-worker. That decision could have been a costly mistake and a major career-derailer.

Vanessa perceived the risk to be greater than the reward. All she focused on was the "what ifs"...what if my mind goes blank, what if I faint on stage, what if I look stupid and incompetent? And, most debilitating of all, what if people find out I'm not perfect? These fears were so overwhelming that Vanessa couldn't appreciate the potential rewards. She had an enormous opportunity to elevate her visibility, take her career to the next level, and deliver a strong professional message on the biggest stage of her career.

After several coaching sessions and some serious soul-searching, Vanessa was willing to feel the fear and do it anyway. She accepted the offer to be the keynote speaker at the conference and none of her "what ifs" came true. Vanessa conquered her fears and didn't allow the power of perfectionism sabotage her opportunity to get ahead.

Leah and Her Presidential Pressure

Vanessa wasn't the only one needing to feel perfectly prepared before accepting an offer. My client, Leah, was a very accomplished family law attorney and partner in her law firm, and actively served on a professional board for years. The current board president's term was ending and another board member nominated Leah for president. Even with an extensive list of accomplishments, Leah felt completely undeserving and under-qualified for the position.

In her mind, she had never held a presidential position before and, therefore, the risk of potential failure was too great. She was convinced that with another year of preparation and some careful planning, she would be perfect for the job. Luckily, she only voiced these concerns with me and we were able to minimize the fears. Eventually, she felt comfortable enough to accept the nomination and, ultimately, accepted the new position as board president.

⌁ Guilty Confession ⌁

At this moment, you are looking squarely at my guilty confession for this sin...this book. I have wanted to write a book for a long time, not only because it brings professional credibility, but because I'm passionate about this topic and would love to reach a wider audience of women. Of course, like many of you, I was waiting until everything was perfect before I put pen to paper... or rather, started typing at my computer.

It's like waiting for the perfect time to have a baby. There is no perfect time. If we all waited for the perfect time to procreate, our species would quickly die out. You never have the perfect amount of money in the bank, are settled into the perfect professional position, or have the perfect parenting plan in place. We would all be childless if we waited for that perfect time.

I don't profess to be a talented writer. In fact, I would prefer to verbally deliver this information to a million women than to write a book for one woman to read. I'm much more confident in my presentation skills than my writing skills, but repeating this message over and over didn't seem to make a lot of sense.

Like most of my clients, I also was committed deeply to the idea of being an "expert" before writing the book and somehow being a successful career coach for 20 years was the magic number. It took two decades of coaching women to greater levels of success before I felt confident enough to call myself an expert. It sounds crazy, and you may be able to relate, but it's true.

My other "perfectionist" hang-up was that I didn't know anything about how to get a book published...therefore, hell was going to freeze over before I ventured into something that had a high degree of risk and was destined to fail. Like most women, I like a "sure thing". I want to have complete control over the process and not knowing is not really an option for me.

"Life is sweetened by risk, so dare to dream big and get comfortable with being uncomfortable. It's only by stepping outside of our safety zone that we truly grow."
—Leeza Gibbons

How ridiculous is this line of thinking? I'm an expert at what I do (yes, I can finally say that with conviction!) and why not trust other experts to do what they do best? I don't have to know everything about everything, and believe me, I don't. The problem is being a natural control freak and admitting to myself, and others, all the things I don't know and asking for help. Not easy for us perfectionists and self-diagnosed control freaks.

I tried to write the book on my own but found myself increasingly frustrated and filled with self-doubt because it wasn't going perfectly. What a shock! I was stuck and simultaneously conflicted. I was passionate about this project and deeply committed to finishing, but it wasn't going as perfectly as I had planned. I finally admitted that I needed help and hired a writing coach. I've been a coach for 20 years, but this was the first time I hired a coach for myself. (It was probably long overdue, but that's another story.)

The mission of this book is to examine how we allow sinful and self-sabotaging behavior derail our success, and I didn't want my desire for perfection to negatively impact this opportunity. My desire to achieve this goal was finally greater than my fear of failing and appearing imperfect. Starting a project and not finishing it felt worse than not having all the answers and asking for help. Coaching a coach is never easy, but I embraced the process and am grateful to my writing coach.

"There came a time when the risk to remain tight in the bud was more painful than the risk it took to blossom."

—Anais Nin

As I was writing this book, I had to constantly remind myself of the goal. The goal wasn't to produce perfection, because that was never going to happen. The goal was to deliver a valuable message in which I could take great pride. It's no small feat to write a book, and if my number one priority was perfection, then it was destined to fail. It would have stayed as ideas in my mind forever and never made it into your hands.

Not only am I working on embracing all the book's imperfections, but also my own. None of us are perfect nor do we really want to be. It's the flaws and imperfections that make use unique and interesting. In fact, I encourage you to find the imperfections in this book, because then you'll know it's real. It's a real expression of my observations, interactions, insights, experience, and heartfelt advice...and it's not perfect!

⤴ Success Solutions ⤴

For my clients who find themselves locked inside the Perfectionism Prison, there are three main strategies I use to help them embrace their imperfections and escape their self-imposed imprisonment.

3 Strategies for Embracing the "Imperfect"

1. Play "What If"
Sometimes the fears and consequences are real, and sometimes they're merely perceived. It's important to know which is which, and the best way to do that is by playing the "what if" game.

If you are waiting for the perfect time to apply for a job or write a book, it will never happen and will then just be another missed opportunity. Instead, think about the "what ifs:"

- *What if* you applied for the job?
- *What if* you only had 80% of the requirements listed on the job description?
- *What if* you got the job or *what if* you didn't get the job?
- *What if* they didn't offer you enough money?
- *What if* the responsibilities were a stretch?
- *What if* you were rejected?
- *What if* only one person reads your book?

Think through all the possible scenarios, good and bad, and play them out to the end. Recognize that an opportunity doesn't have to be perfect to have value. The fear of what might happen is usually greater than what could actually happen. And, trite but true—sometimes it really is about the journey, not the destination.

"When you take risks you learn that there will be times when you succeed and there will be times when you fail, and both are equally important."

—Ellen DeGeneres

2. Take a Risk

If you are paralyzed with fear to step outside your comfort zone and appear imperfect, then this is the exercise for you. If the fear of looking silly or incompetent keeps you from growing and trying new things, then this is *definitely* the exercise for you.

Sometimes taking a big risk at work can be too perilous and carries negative consequences, which is why many women don't do it. The challenge is being able to distinguish a big risk from a small risk. All risks can feel overwhelming and potentially disastrous. That's why many women don't take any risks at all, and that's why they're missing out.

It doesn't always make sense to try to change the risk-taking behavior at work, but what about outside of work? I encourage my "perfect" clients to pick an activity they feel completely insecure about doing, and then do it. They know the outcome won't be perfect; they have to learn how to deal with the discomfort, and then find a way to enjoy the experience along the way.

"Be fearless in trying new things, whether they are physical, mental, or emotional, since being afraid can challenge you to go to the next level."

—Rita Wilson

Here are some of the activities my clients have bravely chosen to do:

- Learning country-western line dancing
- Taking sushi cooking class
- Taking painting class
- Learning a foreign language
- Attending a networking event alone
- Going rock climbing
- Exercising in a Zumba class
- Auditioning for the reality show *Survivor* (that's mine...four times!)

The goal is not to paint like Picasso or to prepare California Rolls like a professional sushi chef; the goal is to realize that even though you may feel completely terrified and uncomfortable, you will survive. You may even enjoy yourself and have fun along the way. Face your fears and do it anyway.

For instance, do I think I could build a perfect fire by rubbing two sticks together, climb a coconut tree or fish for food, or win every physical challenge designed to test the contestants on *Survivor*? Probably not, but I'm willing to try. We only grow when we are truly challenged, and I can't think of a greater challenge then starving on an island with a bunch of strangers for 39 days. I'd give anything for the opportunity to outwit, outplay, and outlast my opponents and win the title of "sole survivor". My bag is packed and I'm still waiting for Jeff Probst (the host) to offer me this once-in-a-lifetime opportunity...call me!

Embracing risk outside of work is a great way to start gaining confidence about taking some risks at work. You may not have complete control about the outcome, but you often have control about the onset. If you want to take your career to the next level, it may be risky and it may not be perfect, but it can be worth it in the end.

3. Burn a Bridge

For our entire lives we've been cautioned to never burn a bridge and that advice has served us well in most cases. But is that always the best advice? If you want to get ahead and you're holding yourself back, it could be time to finally burn a bridge.

In 1519, the Aztec Empire dominated more than 80,000 miles in central and southern Mexico and ruled between 5 and 6 million people. The Spanish Conquistador Hernando Cortes arrived that year with every intention of conquering the powerful empire. To battle the Aztec Empire, Cortes brought with him only 508 soldiers, 100 sailors, and 16 horses.

According to the legend, Cortes burned all the ships after his men arrived on shore. His only strategy was to win or die. He wanted to send a clear message to his men that retreating was not an option. There was no going back and no giving up. The men in his tiny army were literally fighting for their lives, thus intensifying their determination and willingness to fight harder.

Not only did Cortes' army get the message, so did the Aztec soldiers. They knew the Spaniards would fearlessly fight for their lives with nowhere to go but forward. However, the Aztecs could retreat if the fighting became too intense. They still had an "out".

Whether they took the "out" and retreated or were out-battled by the Spanish army, the outcome remains the same:

Cortes and his unfathomably small army conquered the powerful Aztec Empire in 1521.

The lesson is that sometimes you should burn a bridge (or a boat). When retreating or staying stuck in one position is not an option, there is a greater sense of urgency, a deeper commitment, and a stronger determination in surging forward and achieving the goal. There are no excuses, no exit clauses, and failure is off the table. It's full steam ahead without looking back.

> *"Above all, be a heroine of your life, not the victim."*
> **—Nora Ephron**

Burning a bridge (or a boat) also provides an added layer of accountability. You are forced to take action even if it scares you. If you buy a non-refundable membership to a diet program and tell all your friends you're going, you're much more likely to attend the meetings and lose the weight. If you hire a writing coach, submit your manuscript to a publisher, and tell the world you're writing a book, then people will be expecting to see a book. We don't always need to set something on fire to create the sense of urgency and not-so-gentle nudge we often need to get out of our own way and take action.

Not only does that extra layer of accountability help light a fire in your belly, but people see that fire burning. Just like the Aztecs, people know when you are laser-focused and hell-bent on achieving your goal. Sometimes you have to make it impossible to stay still or to retreat in order to make the necessary—yet frightening—moves in your career. Sometimes the best thing you can do is to burn a bridge.

🔺 WOMAN UP! Reflections 🔻

1. Are you trapped inside the "Perfectionism Prison"? Give an example.

_____

_____

_____

_____

_____

_____

2. How has it impacted your career?

_____

_____

_____

_____

_____

_____

_____

3. How do you plan to change it?

_____

_____

_____

_____

_____

_____

_____

Deadly Sin #4
AFFIRMATION ADDICTION

"Success is liking yourself, liking what you do, and liking how you do it."

—*Maya Angelou*

"Go Blue!"

I still cheer for my alma mater and I'm completely convinced that my incessant cheering is what propels the University of Michigan team to victory. When my son received an appointment to the United States

Military Academy at West Point, I started yelling "Go Army!" (Hope it helps them beat Navy.)

There is a reason why cheerleading is such an integral part of our culture. Everyone needs a good cheerleader, a diehard fan, an avid supporter—not just professional sports teams. Cheerleaders are there for support and celebration when you win, and consoling words of encouragement when you lose. "Rah-rah...Go Team, Go!"

But what happens when you can't make a decision at work without that constant cheerleader? What happens when you don't hear "job well done"—is it still a "job well done"? If a tree falls in the forest and no one is there to hear it, does it still make a sound?

Does Someone Need a Hug?

Many women are addicted to affirmation and are easily influenced by the opinions and actions of others. Let's be honest, we all love to hear rave reviews. It's not uncommon for a group of women to get together and the first thing we say is, *"You look amazing! Have you lost weight? That dress is gorgeous, where did you get it?"*

We love compliments. We put a lot of thought and effort into "Girls Night Out", and we love the acknowledgment and squeals of joy. That type of reaction makes us feel really good about the decisions we've made and who we are.

The opposite is also true. If we hear negative or critical feedback, we have a tendency to second-guess ourselves. For instance, you ask your mom or your brutally honest girlfriend (and we all have one...or two!) what she thinks of your newly redecorated living room and she says, "The pillows aren't my favorite."

That reaction can cause some women to rethink those throw pillows and second-guess their own taste and style. *Are those pillows really that awful? I can't believe I thought they looked good in the store. Maybe she has better taste than I do and should rush right out and exchange them? What was I thinking? What else doesn't she like?* It's a slippery slope.

Whether it's a decision about a new hair style or a new hire in your department, that external validation reinforces the fact that you're on the right track, that you made the right decision, that you have good judgment. External validation boosts our confidence and gives us the energy and motivation to keep moving forward. Everyone needs a cheerleader, but the problem occurs when some women rely on that positive feedback so heavily that without it they question their own judgment. They're lost without it.

The need for continuous affirmation can be addictive and may require a 12-step program to break the pattern of behavior.

WOMAN UP! *Tips...*
12 Steps for Breaking the Affirmation Addiction

1. **Consider the source**—*does that person's opinion really matter?*
2. **See the big picture**—*what else is happening outside of your interaction?*
3. **Question the motives**—*what's the other person's agenda?*

4. **Check your sanity**—*ask a trusted source if the criticism is valid.*

5. **Take baby steps**—*take one little step at a time to build self-confidence.*

6. **Trust your gut**—*challenge the feedback if you know it's not true.*

7. **Filter it out**—*listen to the valid criticism and ignore the rest.*

8. **Shift your focus**—*focus on the positive 99% not the negative 1%.*

9. **Keep track**—*keep a Brag Book as a way to remember all the good news.*

10. **Laugh it off**—*don't take every comment and remark so seriously.*

11. **Toughen up**—*business isn't always kind and you can't be so sensitive.*

12. **Celebrate yourself**—*don't wait for someone else to say "good job".*

Jenny and Her Questions

My client, Jenny, was an extremely talented writer and reporter. She had written articles for major magazines and newspapers for more than 10 years. There should have been no question about her skills when it came to writing. However, when Jenny started a new job as the communications director for a small company, she had nothing but questions.

Jenny's job was to develop content and messaging for internal and external communications, but she second-guessed herself and her writing so much she had difficulty even sending out an email. After a few months, Jenny was writing copy to update the company's website and she found herself in her boss' office nearly every day asking, "Is this right? Is this the proper tone? Is this what you're looking for?" Jenny was relying so much on her boss' feedback that she no longer trusted her own instincts and judgment as a professional writer.

Jenny was seeking approval at the micro-level, for every tiny detail, and was asking for her boss's input far too often. She craved constant validation and felt lost without it. Finally, Jenny's boss gave her the input she needed most. Her boss said, "We hired you for your expertise in this area, and I don't have time to review every word you write. I trust you and only want to see the project once it's completed. At that point, we can discuss edits and revisions."

"Take criticism seriously, but not personally. If there is truth or merit in the criticism, try to learn from it. Otherwise, let it roll right off you."

—Hillary Clinton

It's one thing if your boss asks to be kept in the loop on a minute-by-minute basis or is an extreme micro-manager by nature. It's another thing if you find yourself unable to perform your professional responsibilities without ongoing positive feedback...in other words, without your own personal cheerleader.

It's hard for anyone to hear negative comments without feeling criticized or getting defensive. No one likes to feel judged. But, for some reason women are more easily influenced by those external remarks.

For instance, no one really looks forward to their annual performance review. It can feel like an inquisition. You're asked to justify your value to the company, demonstrate how you've met or exceeded expectations, and provide a status report on all goals and objectives. It can be nauseating and nerve-wracking, no doubt.

However, what's amazing is that even when a woman hears a rave review with the highest marks possible and the majority of the comments are positive, she'll still hyper-focus on that one area her boss offered as "room for improvement" or "an opportunity for growth". Why is it that we obsess over the one thing we're not doing well, instead of celebrating all the amazing things we've accomplished?

Carolyn and Her Opportunity for Growth

This is exactly what happened to my client, Carolyn. She managed a call center for a major company and had done an outstanding job for many years. Her boss adored her, she received several promotions, and she was highly respected within the organization. Carolyn went into her annual review expecting to hear nothing but praise and acknowledgment for a job well done. Overall, the review was 99% positive, but her boss suggested she work on her leadership skills and offered to pay for some professional development programs to help improve that skill set.

Carolyn left that meeting feeling completely worthless and second-guessed if she was even doing the right things professionally. Instead of hearing all the glowing remarks that clearly indicated she was an asset to the organization and a valued employee, Carolyn was sent into a downward spiral by that one "opportunity for growth". She even missed the point of the feedback, that the company's willingness to invest in her leadership skills may lead to greater professional opportunities.

"Perfectionists are so used to getting a gold star on their work that receiving negative feedback can be crippling. But instead of viewing criticism as a sign of failure, think of it as an opportunity to learn how to do things better the next time," says Jeff Szymanski, Ph.D., a clinical psychologist. "In other words, embrace your mistakes, so you adapt and grow from them."

"Give yourself the same compassion you extend to others."
—Bonnie Raitt

It's important for women to know that they're doing a great job even if they don't hear it every day, to trust their own judgment that they're making the right decisions, and to be their own cheerleader when they need a little "rah-rah, you can do it!" It's also important to stand your ground when you're being challenged and you know you're right. Don't allow those external influences to cause you to second-guess yourself and don't let them change your mind if it doesn't need changing.

Whose Fault Is it Anyway?

Just as easily as women are externally influenced, they are also quick to internalize failure and blame themselves. Why do we feel we've done something wrong when we haven't? Why do we feel there is something wrong with us that caused a particular outcome? Why do we assume responsibility for things that aren't our fault?

This sinful, self-sabotaging behavior is best illustrated by every woman's least favorite activity...jeans shopping. (Did you think I would say swimsuit shopping? That's a little too personal and traumatic!) A woman will walk into a fitting room with 10 pairs of jeans and walk out with none because none of them fit and she's in tears. She tells herself the jeans don't fit because, "*My butt's too big, my legs are too short, and my muffin-top is an affront to society.*" Obviously there is something seriously wrong with her body, and it's totally her fault that she doesn't own a decent pair of jeans.

In contrast, a man walks into a fitting room with 10 pairs of jeans and walks out with none, and his internal dialogue is very different. He tells himself, "*There must be something wrong with these stupid jeans. Their design isn't right. Why don't manufacturers know how to make a decent pair of jeans now-a-*

days?" A man has no trouble deflecting blame while women willingly accept all the blame.

Taking ownership and responsibility is a sign of strong leadership and good character, but it can backfire if you assume everything is your fault.

"The truth will set you free. But first, it will piss you off."
—Gloria Steinem

Using a more professional example, I have male and female job-seekers in my practice and it's fascinating how differently they perceive rejection. If a male client is not offered a job, he's quick to say, "*It's their loss. They missed out on an amazing catch.*" If a female client is not offered a job, she will usually ask, "*What did I do wrong? What's the matter with me?*" A man will blame the misguided hiring manager while a woman will blame herself.

Lisa and Her Demons

My client, Lisa, spent years working in a hostile and unhealthy work environment. She was abused relentlessly by a co-worker who was determined to sabotage her career. However, the co-worker was sneaky and careful not to exhibit the abusive behavior in front of others. She was ruthless when it came to office politics, spreading untrue rumors about Lisa, undermining her authority, stealing her ideas, and taking credit for Lisa's work.

Instead of Lisa clearly being able to recognize her co-worker's "not-so-hidden" agenda, she internalized the behavior and blamed herself. She thought, "I must have done something wrong to make her so mad. Why else would she be acting like this?" Lisa also thought she could fix the situation by befriending her co-worker, by working harder, by being a "better" co-worker herself. What Lisa hadn't considered was that it was her co-worker who was responsible for the toxic work environment, not her.

Lisa finally hit rock bottom. She was depressed, started losing her hair, and even developed a painful stomach condition. Knowing that her demonic co-worker was a permanent fixture within the organization, Lisa had to muster up enough confidence and energy to pursue another job. It wasn't until she was happily employed at another company, and had some distance and perspective, that she could reflect back and analyze the situation. Eventually, Lisa was able to see her former co-worker's true colors and how she tried to sabotage her career. Lisa vowed to never allow someone else to hold that much power over her again.

WOMAN UP! *Tips…*
Subtle Signs Your Co-Worker May Be a Saboteur

1. *She cleverly hoards information that you need to complete your assignment.*
2. *She "forgets" to send you an invitation to the meeting.*

3. *She acts one way with you and another way in front of everyone else.*
4. *She repeatedly sets you up for failure, not success.*
5. *She throws you under the bus faster than she defends you.*

Dina and Her Moody Manager

Another client, Dina, experienced a similar situation with her manager. Dina held her breath and walked around on eggshells until she could determine her manager's "mood-of-the-day". If he was in a good mood, Dina was in a good mood. If he was in a bad mood, Dina was miserable and blamed herself. She was so easily influenced by his temperament that she allowed it to negatively impact her performance and sabotage her career within the company.

She doubted her own judgment and felt worthless. She didn't believe she could do anything right. It never occurred to her that her manager's mood had nothing to do with her, and that he just had a crabby personality and poor managerial skills. Dina received the best news when her manager was transferred to another department and she started working for a much less moody manager.

"The most common way people give up their power is by thinking they don't have any."

—Alice Walker

External forces and voices will always have an impact on our personal and professional lives. It's up to us to properly filter the information in a way that's helpful and not harmful. Paying too much attention, and placing too much importance and emphasis on others' affirmations, can kill your career. Giving your power away is never an option... *WOMAN UP!* and be your own cheerleader.

⌐ Guilty Confession ⌐

As much as I would like to think that the opinions of other don't matter, the reality is that they do. I have an intense aversion to judgment and criticism just like everyone else. Publishing this book for all to read (including professional book reviewers and critical bloggers) has been a tremendous test in bravery and vulnerability for me.

I am actually guilty of committing this sin multiple times throughout my career. For example, I have been a public speaker delivering presentations for years—and I love it. It's one of my favorite activities and I feel very confident about my ability to deliver a message and connect with an audience. I have also been fortunate to have received a lot of positive praise and feedback.

Early on, there was a woman I admired who was a paid, national, keynote speaker. At the time, these were all the goals I was trying to achieve in my career...especially the "paid" part. In my mind, she was a speaking "goddess" and was clearly doing everything right. I was in awe of this woman and greatly admired everything she had done.

One day we happened to be speaking at the same event, but on different topics. I was delivering a career-related presentation and she spoke about technology and social media. After the event, I approached her like an adoring fan and confessed my deep admiration for all that she had accomplished.

She was gracious and appreciative and offered to give me some advice. Of course I was dying to hear what she had to say. My intention was to be a sponge and soak up every ounce of wisdom she was willing to share. She began by complimenting me on my content, industry expertise, organization of the information, and energetic and entertaining delivery style. However, she suggested I incorporate more personal stories into my presentations to make the content more relatable if I wanted to take my public speaking career to the "next level".

Of course all I heard was, "*You're a horrible speaker and there are major elements lacking in your presentations. You'll never make it in this business!*" I completely ignored all the nice things she said and only focused on the one piece of constructive feedback she was kind enough to offer. I was devastated and seriously questioned whether I should ever speak another word in public again.

After I calmed down, I took an honest inventory of my public speaking skills and thought about her advice. I really enjoyed listening to other speakers when they told stories, so maybe it was a technique I could use to make my presentations even better.

"You don't become what you want, you become what you believe."

—Oprah Winfrey

I had an emotional and defensive reaction to her feedback and could have easily discounted her advice and continued on with my same old presentation style. It also could have rocked my confidence to the point where I retired from public speaking forever. Fortunately, I had enough sense to not allow either of those options to come to fruition.

Even though I am innately a very private person, I embraced her wisdom and decided to venture into the pool of vulnerability. I started sharing more personal stories, lessons I've learned, challenges I've overcome, and sins I've committed. She was right and the response has been overwhelming. People do relate better to stories, they remember the anecdotes, and they feel a deeper sense of connection to you and the information.

As a writer, I have also used her advice to connect with my readers...and it has paid off in ways I could never have imagined. I dedicate this chapter and all the "Guilty Confessions" to that public speaking "goddess" who influenced me more than she'll ever know. You helped me *Woman UP!* Thank you.

↗ Success Solutions ↖

Knowing how important external validation and support are, what happens if you don't have that cheerleader with you at work? Do you allow your career goals to crumble? Do you doubt your ability to contribute and make a difference? Of course not! It's time to be your own BFF (best friends forever) at work.

"When a woman becomes her own best friend life is easier."
—Diane Von Furstenberg

For women, the only thing better than a great group of girlfriends is one BFF. One of the most famous and well-known friendships is the one between Oprah and her BFF, Gayle. Oprah has described Gayle as, "The mother I never had. She is the sister everybody would want. She is the friend that everybody deserves. I don't know a better person."

The positive impact of a BFF is not only anecdotal, but also scientific. According to a study published in the *Journal of Experimental Social Psychology*, researchers asked participants to stand at the base of a mountain and estimate how hard it would be to climb. Those participants standing with a friend estimated the mountain to be less steep compared to those standing alone. The study showed that the longer the friendship, the less steep they estimated the incline. The power of friendship could literally turn a mountain into a molehill.

Even if you're not standing at the base of a mountain, a BFF can be a tremendous asset. According to Oprah, a best friend "wants the best for you in every single situation of your life. Lifts you up. Supports you. Always!" This is the unwritten contract that exists between best friends and gives the relationship so much meaning and enduring strength.

It's easy to see why women cherish these relationships. It makes us better people and enriches our lives. But what if you don't work with your BFF? How do you get the support and encouragement you often need without your best friend in the next office? There are many lessons to be learned from this powerful friendship, and if we apply them to ourselves, we can thrive and be our own BFF at work.

Yes, it's nice to have a BFF working with you in the same office, but it can also become a crutch. Relying on yourself and becoming your own BFF will ultimately prove to be the greatest gift you can give yourself.

6 Benefits of Being Your Own BFF

1. See Clearly

Sometimes it's hard to see people for who they really are, and we're often too quick to give someone the benefit of the doubt. If your co-worker or manager is making your life miserable, don't jump to the conclusion that you are the one who did something wrong. Your best friend would pull a Cher move from *Moonstruck*, slap you in the face and say, "Snap out of it!" She would help you see the reality of the situation, analyze the toxic behavior, and then say, "She's the crazy one, not you." Sometimes you just need to slap yourself and see things more clearly.

2. Stay Committed

Unfortunately, when we receive some not-so-favorable feedback and start doubting ourselves, our first impulse is to abandon ship and throw in the towel. We question whether or not we'd be better off doing something else. Sometimes that is the answer, but more often it's best to take the feedback with a grain of salt and stay the course. Part of the reason why your best friend holds that special place in your heart is because she is committed and loyal to the end. She doesn't give up on you and get another BFF after a bad day, and neither should you. Dig deep and stay committed.

3. Celebrate Success

Women can barely recognize—much less celebrate—their own successes. They are viewed as just "part of the job" or "no big deal". What a BFF would congratulate and celebrate is what you might gloss over and minimize. A BFF would give you a huge hug and then take you out for margaritas, because she knows how hard you worked and how badly you really wanted that promotion. It's a highly competitive environment and women need to own their accomplishments. Celebrate your successes, no matter how big or small, just as your best friend would.

4. Dismiss Self-Doubt

As we discussed before, women want to have 100% of the new job description or promotion qualifications and a 100% guarantee of the outcome before moving forward. Women will hyper-focus on that one skill they don't have and will allow self-doubt to creep in and prevent them from optimizing a golden opportunity. A BFF would tell you to go for it! Your best friend would point out how amazing and spectacular you are and how the rest of the candidates can't hold a candle to you. Your best friend sees the best in you even when you can't see it. Be your own BFF and give yourself the extra boost of confidence when you need it most. You can do it!

5. Practice Forgiveness

The only thing that lasts longer than holding a grudge against someone else are the grudges we hold against ourselves. A woman will agonize for weeks because she mistakenly hit "reply all" to an email, forgot to bring the report to the meeting, or called a client by the wrong name. Your best friend would laugh, make you laugh, and then tell you *"It's no big deal in the grand scheme of things."* If women could let go a little and give themselves the perspective they need and the forgiveness they deserve, they would be much better off at work.

6. Release Perfectionism

Women have an innate aversion to appearing incompetent, unprepared, or uninformed—especially at work. It's critical for women to maintain that perfect façade, only take very calculated risks, and be able to predict or to control the outcome. No surprises. The result is that women often miss out on opportunities and they don't challenge themselves the same way men do. A BFF would remind you that the best adventures you ever had were when things didn't go perfectly or according to plan, that you had the time of your life when the unexpected happened. Release the myth that perfect even exists and embrace that fact that imperfect can often be even better.

WOMAN UP! *Tips…*
The Best Qualities of your Best Friend

1. *She is your greatest cheerleader.*
2. *She always sees and brings out the best in you.*
3. *She is honest and forgiving.*
4. *She is brave when you are scared.*
5. *She is strong when you are weak.*
6. *She is the voice of reason when you feel crazy.*
7. *She makes you laugh when all you want to do is cry.*
8. *She knows you're not perfect and loves you even more.*
9. *She will celebrate and remind you of your successes.*
10. *She will defend you until the end.*

Wanting the best for your BFF is natural. Being your own BFF sometimes is not. However, if you commit to being as good to yourself as you are to your best friend, then you'll both have a lot to celebrate. Be your own best friend and tell yourself to *WOMAN UP!*

♪ WOMAN UP! Reflections ↳

1. Do you suffer from "Affirmation Addiction"? Give an example.

   _____

   _____

   _____

   _____

   _____

   _____

2. How has it impacted your career?

   _____

   _____

   _____

   _____

   _____

   _____

   _____

3. How do you plan to change it?

   _____

   _____

   _____

   _____

   _____

   _____

Deadly Sin #5
DIVULGENCE DISEASE

"Words have power—the power to inspire and guide us, touch our hearts, even change the way we look at our lives."

—*Maria Shriver*

As women, rarely are we at a loss for words. We love to talk, chat, share, commiserate, gossip, text, post, and tweet. The issue isn't whether or not we are hard-wired to communicate, but rather that we communicate too much. The question then becomes, is our communication helping or hurting us? Is it saving or sabotaging our careers?

Show Up and Throw Up

Some could argue that our greatest sin is that we overshare and "show up and throw up". When you first meet someone, do you reveal too much too soon? Do you tell an acquaintance your life story without even being asked?

My mom is the poster-child for oversharing. My grandfather was having heart surgery years ago, and I was in the waiting room with my mom, my grandmother, and my sister. Within minutes my mom was swapping medical stories and contact information with complete strangers waiting anxiously to hear about their own loved ones.

My mom also is incapable of shopping at a store in Denver (where I live), and not telling the cashier that she really lives in Chicago and is just visiting her daughter and grandchildren. It's not as if the cashier is asking her any of these probing questions, but my mom can't resist the impulsive urge to share her story.

We also all have someone (or many people) in our lives that feel the need to incessantly share every detail of their lives on social media. Every meal is photographed and posted, every thought is exposed, and every funny cartoon or quote is shared. There are people who seemingly operate without an appropriate filter or censor.

Words are powerful tools and should be used with extreme caution and careful consideration. Our parents were right when they tried to teach us to "think before we speak". (Ok, maybe not my mom.) Once your words are out there, you can't take them back. You don't get to hit rewind and start over, and a heartfelt apology sometimes is insufficient to undo the damage that impulsive statements can make.

"Share with people who've earned the right to hear your story."

—Dr. Brené Brown

Robin and Her Reckless Weakness

My favorite example of this Deadly Sin is in the mock interview session I had with my client, Robin. Robin was a marketing professional in her mid-twenties and was trying to find a new job. She had no trouble securing the first interview but was rarely invited back for a second interview. She couldn't understand why. We sat down to do a mock interview to see if I could detect any major red flags in her answers. Was there something she was saying that caused her to be eliminated from the interviewing process so early?

I asked her the standard, and not so standard, interviewing questions and then we got to the classic interviewing question: "What's your greatest weakness?" This question is so well-worn, so over-tried and true, that every job seeker should be prepared to answer it. It's asked in almost every interview in one way or another, so it shouldn't be a surprise.

I asked Robin about her "greatest weakness" and her response was, "I have difficulty getting to work on time." I was completely shocked by her answer and thought I was on an episode of Candid Camera or, today, Punk'd. I asked if that was really how she answered the question in an actual interview, and she said, "Yes, because it's the truth."

I would never advise anyone to lie in an interview. However, there are plenty of other true "weakness" answers that won't do as much damage as Robin's honest answer. In those eight simple words, the hiring managers saw Robin as irresponsible, apathetic, and unreliable with a poor work ethic. No wonder she was rarely asked back for another interview. When I explained to Robin how her answer could be interpreted and how she was being perceived, she was shocked. She hadn't thought about it from the hiring manager's perspective before.

To help Robin improve her interviewing skills, we examined her other "weaknesses" and strategically selected one that wouldn't automatically get her eliminated from the process. Interviewing is an intense example of how critical it is to think ahead and choose your words carefully. There isn't always a new job on the line, but impulsively speaking before you think could impact the outcome of other situations such as managing a major project or closing a big deal.

I have coached hundreds of women and have found that most women are crystal clear on what they're *not* good at. They are quick to rattle off the entire laundry list of weaknesses while they struggle to articulate a single strength. That needs to change.

Not only do women have a tendency to answer honestly and overshare when asked a direct question, but also when an indirect question is posed. It's as if women are waiting for an opportunity to tell you what they're not good at before they mention what they are good at. It's true that women bond by sharing experiences and being self-deprecating, but that doesn't always serve us well in the workplace.

Laura and Her True Confession

I was on a committee with several other women and the committee chair asked who would like to present the updated information at the next meeting. Laura quickly announced, "I could never do that. I get so nervous speaking in front of a crowd, I'm afraid I would pass out." For some reason she felt compelled to divulge the skills she felt most insecure about, instead of volunteering for the activities that gave her the highest degree of confidence.

Laura is a master at organization, is extremely detail-oriented, and takes the most amazing minutes I've ever seen. Those are the skills she should have highlighted first and the responsibilities for which she should have proudly volunteered.

Just because you share your deepest, darkest secrets, fears, dreams, and anxieties with your girlfriends doesn't mean it's always appropriate to share with your work friends. And, yes, there is a difference. People at work have their own goals and agendas, and sharing too much personal information too soon can sabotage your career. It's not pleasant to think about, but people can, and will, use information against you if it will further their own interests.

Patty and Her Painful Email

My client, Patty, learned this lesson the hard way. She was having a very difficult time adjusting to her new boss after her previous boss retired. For some reason, they just did not get along and Patty found herself increasingly frustrated and at odds with her boss' management style. On a particularly bad day, Patty vented to her co-worker in an email about her true feelings towards her boss. Patty thought she and the co-worker were good friends and in agreement that the new boss was a "raging lunatic".

A few weeks later, Patty's boss called her into a meeting. Somehow the new boss "discovered" the less-than-complimentary email and confronted Patty about it. Of course, Patty never intended for him to see it and found herself in a very defensive and awkward position. The result was that it damaged their relationship beyond repair and Patty was forced to look for a new job.

What Happens in Vegas...

The same scenario is true about everyone's favorite online pastime: Facebook and social media. Unfortunately, what happens in Vegas doesn't always stay in Vegas, especially if you post it online. Your online presence is available for anyone and everyone to see including current managers, prospective hiring managers, admissions officers, co-workers, subordinates, clients, fellow volunteers, and other professional colleagues. Not only do you need to think before you speak, but you also need to think before you post.

Oversharing online is a deal-breaker, a career-killer, and a dangerous self-sabotaging sin. It's especially dangerous when you post late at night, impulsively out of anger, or subconsciously without thinking. Social media is a fantastic way to stay connected by sharing news and photos with friends and family, but keep in mind that words are powerful tools that can either help you, hurt you, or come back to haunt you.

Molly and Her Trip to Mexico

My client, Molly, had aspirations of moving up the ladder in the field of corporate health and wellness. She had worked very hard, received additional certifications, and finally made it to the last step in the interviewing process for her dream job.

While the decision-makers were making their final decision, Molly took a trip to Mexico with her girlfriends. She was thinking of the trip as a pre-celebration to the job offer she was sure to receive upon her return. Molly and her girlfriends took the celebration to another level, and one margarita turned into many, and the entire jubilant affair was captured on several iPhones for posterity.

Molly never posted the pictures on Facebook, but her girlfriends did and they "tagged" her in the pictures. A woman who had dedicated her professional life to clean and healthy living now appeared as a complete contradiction. Of course, the hiring managers did their research and found the pictures. They felt that Molly's online image was not aligned with the image of the position, and they questioned her ability to authentically represent the organization. The offer went to another candidate and Molly learned a very valuable lesson.

◢ Guilty Confession ◣

I am not an overly revealing woman by nature. In fact, I probably err on the side of not sharing enough. I am a pretty private person and am careful about what I share and with whom I share it. If truth be told, I resisted engaging in any social media activity as long as I could, because it made me feel too exposed and vulnerable.

As I'm writing this, I realize how paranoid I sound. But it's true. I am much more comfortable sitting in the coaching chair and listening to my clients than sharing my own life story. These guilty confessions may not seem like a big deal to most, but it's my way of being a little more sinful and stepping outside my own comfort zone.

However, I have been guilty of "speaking before thinking" in my personal life. Remember, I was a very stubborn and fiercely independent child and often blurted out statements that I was forced to defend. My grandparents always said I would "cut off my nose to spite my face". In other words, if I argued that it wasn't that cold outside, I would force myself to brave a blizzard without a coat. If I told a boyfriend that we were done and no longer speaking, hell would freeze over before I uttered another word to him. It's certainly not my best quality, but I did learn a valuable lesson the hard way.

When my son, Zachary, was exerting his power as a cantankerous, disagreeable three-year-old, I would start off the day with a plethora of effective parenting strategies and coping skills. By the end of the day, I was an exhausted, delirious mess of a mom. I was reduced to threatening his very existence and the items and activities he cherished the most.

In a sleep-deprived state of mind, because I also had a newborn daughter, Rachel, who refused to sleep through the night, I snapped one day and told Zachary that if he didn't cooperate (I don't remember the exact crime he committed) I would take away his television-viewing privileges for an entire week. Before I knew what happened, the words were out of my mouth and the deed was done. I made a promise to myself, and my children, that I would always do what I said I was going to do. It was a "mommy-integrity" oath I took very seriously the day my first child was born.

The good news is that Zachary learned early on that I did not make idle threats. The bad news is that I suffered through seven painstakingly quiet days without his favorite television shows (Barney, Rugrats, Blue's Clues, Thomas the Tank Engine, and Arthur) as distractions. In a way, we all learned a valuable lesson. My children knew that I was a mommy of my word... and I learned (or relearned) to think before I speak.

Not only has this lesson served me well as a mom, but also as a professional. I don't make promises to my clients I can't keep. I don't post or send an email without assuming it is public knowledge. And I don't trust someone with valuable information until they've earned my trust. I know there have been a few blunders throughout my career, but I try to remember the consequences of my actions when I speak before I think.

◢ Success Solutions ◣

If you are guilty of revealing too much too soon, over-divulging, oversharing information, speaking or sharing before you think, or TMI (too much information), then it's time to practice a little impulse control and start "overthinking" and obeying some simple rules.

Knowing what you want to say ahead of time and practicing it is the only thing that keeps the mind from going blank. Or worse, saying the wrong thing. Whether you are preparing for a board meeting, an annual review, a presentation, a networking event, or a job interview, knowing what you want to say, and what you DON'T want to say, is the best strategy for combating this self-sabotaging sin.

5 Simple Rules to Prevent TMI

1. Know Your Audience
Being able to distinguish friend from foe is a virtue in the workplace. Does that person have your back or will that person use the information against you? Ladies, we are blessed with amazing intuition and insight...use it. If that little voice is cautioning you about a co-worker, believe it. Don't be so quick

to dismiss the warning signs and grant that person the benefit of the doubt. Let the other person earn your trust before you give it.

2. Lead with the Positive
Regardless of the situation, always lead with something positive before you start bringing out all the skeletons from your closet. That way, you have a chance to keep the bus moving positively rather than throwing yourself under it. Also, take a moment to notice how different the reaction is when a comment is made with self-confidence versus one made with self-deprecation. No one knows everything, but you do know something. Lead with what you know and with what you feel most confident about.

3. Take a Breath
There is nothing wrong with taking a thoughtful and contemplative pause before you blurt out your answer. For a lot of "over-sharers", speaking before thinking can be a nervous reaction. You simply say the first thing that pops into your head to try to avoid an awkward silence. An awkward silence is always better than TMI and there is always time to take a breath.

4. Script It Out
Actors use a script to deliver their message on target...why shouldn't you? Even the greatest actors like Meryl Streep and Robert DeNiro start with a script and get comfortable with the words before they take the stage or appear on screen. Scripting out your message ahead of time may not win you an

"Oscar", but it will definitely help increase your awareness of how powerful your words really are. Speaking points keep you on point.

5. Stay Silent

When in doubt, stay silent. If you're not sure what to say, how to say it, or who to say it to, silence will always serve you well. There are plenty of other verbose individuals who will be happy to talk all day long, so let them. Being an active listener is an important skill in the workplace, and most people would be better off if they spent more time listening than speaking anyway.

"Listening is becoming a lost art—practice it."
—Nancy McFadden

According to the International Listening Association, "We listen at 125-250 words per minute, but think at 1,000-3,000 words per minute. Immediately after we listen to someone, we only recall about 50% of what they said. More than 35 business studies indicate that listening is a top skill needed for success in business." As George Burns said in the 1977 movie, *Oh God*, "I can't help hearing. I don't always listen."

Not only can your words do some major damage in person, but they can be downright lethal online. At least in person if you're guilty of TMI, you can hope the other person didn't hear you or suffers from short-term memory loss, but once it's online it lives in cyber-space forever. Your online presence not only represents you and your brand, but it's there for all to see and for all eternity.

If you're in career transition or thinking about making a career move, it is important to know that CareerBuilder's 2013 survey showed that 43% (I personally think that's trending much higher today) of hiring managers have used content from social media sites that caused them NOT to hire a particular candidate. Here's what they found and how it impacted their decision:

- 50% found provocative and/or inappropriate photos or information
- 48% found information about drinking or drug use
- 33% found the candidate bad-mouthing a previous employee, colleague, or client
- 30% found the candidate had poor communication skills
- 28% found discriminatory remarks relating to race, gender, or religion
- 24% found the candidate lied about qualifications

If you carelessly overshare on social media sites it can definitely cause a hiring manager to think twice and eliminate you from consideration, but sharing information strategically can actually work in your favor. In the same survey, nearly one in five hiring managers (19%) admitted to finding information online that led to hiring a candidate. Here's the proof:

- 57% found the information to convey a professional image
- 50% found the information to convey a good feel for the candidate's personality
- 50% found the information to show the candidate was well-rounded with a wide range of interests
- 49% found the information to support the candidate's professional qualifications
- 46% found the information to show the candidate was creative
- 43% found the information to show the candidate had great communication skills
- 38% found positive references/recommendations posted about the candidate

Posting pictures, comments, and cartoons on Facebook and other social media sites has become part of our social lexicon. It's an acceptable and preferable form of communication for millions of people. There is no escaping social media today...it's here to stay. The question is, is your social media activity and online presence helping you or hurting you?

Sharing with others is a wonderful quality when done appropriately and professionally. Keep in mind that not only are your friends and family paying attention to your posts, but so is your boss or manager. If you want to stay employed, you may want to think before you post. Here's what your boss will know about you from your online activity:

- That you were posting online during working hours when you should have been working
- That you went on a ranting rampage about your boss, company, co-workers, or clients
- That you have many dirty little secrets and odd "likes"
- That you were lying when you "called in sick"
- That you have extreme social or political beliefs

As a general rule, if you wouldn't say it to your boss's face, then don't post it online. And if you do, then you'll have no one to blame but yourself if that information comes back to bite you. It's always better to be safe than sorry. In order to help those that have a tendency to reveal too much too soon, here is a universal list of taboo topics to avoid discussing, sharing, announcing, and posting at work.

WOMAN UP! *Tips…*
Top 10 Taboo Topics to Share at Work

1. *You're interviewing for another job.*
2. *Your political views and who you're voting for in the next election.*
3. *Your religious views and opinions about other religions.*
4. *Your negative feelings about your boss, co-workers, clients and company.*
5. *Your paycheck and the paycheck of others.*

6. *Your recreational drug and drinking habits.*
7. *Your sex life and favorite scenes from 50 Shades of Grey.*
8. *Your goal of moving into the corner office that's currently occupied.*
9. *Your personal drama with a spouse, girl/boyfriend, or children.*
10. *Your previous or current medical issues.*

I am not suggesting that you remain tight-lipped forever and never share a personal thought or amusing anecdote. Building relationships at work is important and represents a critical component to professional success and mobility. I'm merely suggesting that you take your time, allow the trusted relationships to form naturally, and think twice before divulging too much too soon.

In order to successfully *WOMAN UP!,* sometimes the best thing we can do is slow down and keep our secrets a secret.

♦ WOMAN UP! Reflections ♦

1. Are you suffering from the "Divulgence Disease"? Give an example.

   _____

   _____

   _____

   _____

   _____

   _____

2. How has it impacted your career?

   _____

   _____

   _____

   _____

   _____

   _____

3. How do you plan to change it?

   _____

   _____

   _____

   _____

   _____

   _____

Deadly Sin #6
MISCOMMUNICATION MAYHEM

"As women we have the opportunity to lift up other women through words, deeds, and intentions."

—Jess Weiner

M any agree that verbal communication is the trait that distinguishes humans from animals, and we have already discussed how much women love verbal communication. Many also agree that 93% of all communication is non-verbal. Regardless of whether or not you agree with scientific studies and statistics, the truth is that communication is the key to success.

But do you know what message you're really communicating?

We have all heard the old adage that "you only have one chance to make a first impression". And, it's a fact that a first impression is made within the first seven seconds. Even for a fast-talker, seven seconds is not a lot of time, so the majority of the first impression is based on non-verbal communication cues. It's crucial to recognize and be aware of what your presence and body language say about you. Does your body language say you're confident or cautious? Personable or passive? Timid or on top of the world?

Harvard social psychologist, Amy Cuddy, has documented how positive and negative body language shapes your self-perceptions and your hormone levels. In Cuddy's experiment, conducted in collaboration with Dana Carney at Berkeley, one group spent two minutes doing "low-power" poses: head down, shoulders sunk, eyes averted, looking small. The other group performed "high-power" poses: hands on hips, chest lifted, staring boldly out at the horizon a la Wonder Woman.

Then they took a saliva sample. The high-power posers showed a nearly 20% increase in testosterone (the dominance hormone) and a 25% decrease in cortisol (the stress hormone). The low-power posers saw a 10% decline in testosterone and a 17% increase in cortisol.

Cuddy concludes, "These two-minute changes [in body stance] lead to hormonal changes that can configure your brain to be either assertive, confident and comfortable, or really stress reactive and feeling shut down."

Often you create that first impression before you even say hello. Yes, it's based on criticism and judgment, preconceived ideas, and unfair biases. But that's reality and that's how critical your physical presence is in a professional environment. Your body language can communicate—but it can also miscommunicate. It's up to you. *WOMAN UP!*

What does your body language say about you?

Physical Messages and Mishaps

1. A Handshake

It's customary to greet someone and to introduce yourself with a handshake, but what message is your handshake really sending? Many women do themselves an enormous disservice by having a weak handshake…otherwise known as the dreaded "dead-fish" handshake. Nothing will leave a worse impression than a limp, flimsy, poor-excuse-of-a-handshake. The assumption is that a weak handshake equals a weak woman.

Felicity and Her Feeble Handshake

My client, Felicity, was a very successful attorney who was in the process of looking for another position. As with all job seekers, Felicity spent a lot of time networking and meeting people, and that usually meant a lot of hand-shaking. At our first meeting, I realized that she had one of the weakest handshakes I'd ever encountered. It was uncomfortable, distracting, and memorable in the worst kind of way. It even elicited a physical response, like when sour milk leaves a bad taste in your mouth; every time you think of it, your stomach turns and the small hairs on your neck stand up.

In addition to discussing job search strategies, résumé formats, and interviewing skills, we also spent a considerable amount of time practicing a stronger handshake. She had no idea the negative message she was sending with her limp handshake. Practice makes "perfect" and Felicity's handshake greatly improved.

The flipside, obviously, is when women try to overcompensate with the "bone-crusher" handshake. I realize the intention is to send a strong, authoritative message, but there is no need to bring someone to their knees to show your dominance. It's inappropriate and off-putting. This is not the kind of first impression you want to make.

2. Direct Eye Contact and a Smile

Eye contact sends a direct and confident message in the business world. For women, it's not the time to be coy and bat your eyes. Avoiding eye contact will weaken your position and give an unimpressive first impression. Holding someone's gaze is as important as holding your ground. The eyes are thought to be the windows to your soul, and if you have nothing to hide, then let them see who you really are. Try out some direct eye contact and get a feel for how long a held gaze stays comfortable (studies suggest 2-3 seconds).

The other non-verbal communication cue that people take notice of right away is your smile. However, there is a big difference between an authentic and an inauthentic smile and people can tell the difference. Sometimes women will smile excessively out of nervousness or a desire to appear polite. This may cast doubt on their professionalism in serious situations. A warm, comfortable smile shows you feel good about yourself and are happy to be there.

3. Dress Code

In addition to your handshake, eye contact, and smile, most people will take notice of your physical appearance and will make certain judgments based on how you look. No, it's not fair, but it is reality. Does your professional image send the right message?

Becky and Her Bursting Bag

As a recruiter, I was working with a national pharmaceutical company to fill a sales position that covered a five-state territory. Becky was an ideal candidate, a great match for the organization, and was sailing through the interviewing process. In her last interview, she met with the vice president of sales, and dressed as impeccably as she had before.

As she sat down for the interview, she placed her suitcase-sized purse on the floor and it burst open. What the hiring manager saw was a disorganized mess, and his assumption was that if her purse was this disorganized then she clearly lacked the necessary organizational skills to perform the job. In his eyes, a messy purse was a deal-killer.

Yes, the judgment is harsh and the verdict is swift, but that's how quickly and definitively people make up their minds. Everything about you communicates perceived and actual messages, and you have the power to manage and to minimize Miscommunication Mayhem.

4. Weak and Overly-Familiar Body Language

Body language and gestures can have different meanings for different genders. Women will nod their heads to indicate understanding and active listening. Men interpret head-nodding as a sign of agreement. It's the same with shoulder-shrugging. Women will shrug their shoulders as a cute, playful gesture, while men believe shoulder-shrugging is a sign that you don't know the answer. Be aware of your body language and what it's saying to your audience, otherwise it can turn into Miscommunication Mayhem.

Women are natural huggers, not hand-shakers. Giving someone a hug hello in your personal life is totally appropriate. It's not always appropriate in your professional life. Being overly familiar and demonstrative with physical contact in the workplace can be misinterpreted as flirtatious and overtly sexual. You appear as someone who doesn't understand boundaries and proper professional etiquette. Better safe than sorry...always lead with a handshake and wait and see if the relationship appropriately evolves into a hug.

5. No Crying in the Office

Just like Tom Hanks exclaimed in the 1992 film *A League of Their Own*—"*There's no crying baseball!*"—there's also no crying allowed in business. Women already have to combat the "overly emotional" argument as to why we don't make strong enough leaders, so you certainly don't want to provide any additional ammunition. Without even saying a word, crying at work makes you look weak and unstable.

There are times when issues do get emotional at work, but there is a difference between genuine emotion and emotional manipulation. It's never in your best interest to let others see you cry excessively in the workplace. That's what bathrooms are for. Crying at work makes other people feel uncomfortable and it weakens your position.

Christine and Her Crier

My client, Christine, was a manager in an insurance office. She was a wonderful leader and operated with a lot of compassion and understanding. However, she had one female employee who cried nearly every time Christine provided her with feedback. She was incredibly sensitive and her crying caused Christine so much anxiety and discomfort that she didn't believe she could effectively manage her. Christine's strategy was to avoid her as much as possible and, as a result, the subordinate's career really suffered. She didn't receive the same guidance and professional development opportunities that were offered to her co-workers. Her inability to control her tears caused others to question her ability to manage a more challenging workload.

6. Sit Up and Stand Tall

When you're in a meeting, have you ever noticed how much space men occupy? They're all spread out with papers and folders strewn about and their arms wide open. Women, on the other hand, naturally try to take up as little space as possible. We have neat little piles in front of us and often sit with our hands in our laps or our arms crossed.

That body language says, "*Don't look at me, I'm insignificant.*" It's as if you're trying to fade into the background and to not draw a lot of attention to yourself. Understandably, the goal for many women is to not look bigger than they are. This makes sense when it comes to health and a positive body image, but that same mindset can sabotage us in the workplace.

Slouching your shoulders, folding your hands in your lap, and crossing your ankles when standing are all gestures that convey a lack of confidence and subordination. Without saying a word, you can tell someone a lot about how you're feeling and your status within an organization.

Think about your body language the next time you're in a meeting and ask yourself, "*Am I shrinking away or standing tall?*" A confident posture is the sign of a confident woman.

"*Dress shabbily and they remember the dress; dress impeccably and they remember the woman.*"

—Coco Chanel

Even though it's politically incorrect to talk about the shallow reality of clothing and a woman's appearance, we must. I hear all the time that what really matters "is what's on the inside", and as much as we'd all like that to be true, it's not. The clothing choices you make and the professional image you're creating say everything about your brand, your status within an organization or in the community, and how successful you are (or are trying to be).

Your appearance is important not only in establishing a positive first impression, but it's a critical component to the successful trajectory of your career. There is great value in the idea that you should dress for the position you want, not the one you have. Again, it's not politically correct, but it is true. Whether you're interviewing for a new job, meeting a prospective client, or seeking to climb the corporate ladder, be aware of the message your professional image is sending. Your image has the power to skyrocket or sabotage your career. It's up to you.

Heather and Her Hippy-Look

My client, Heather, was a brilliant engineer and had her sights set on an ultra-conservative aerospace organization as her next career move. Not only was Heather a genius, but she loved her hippy wardrobe. She was gorgeous but looked like she stepped out of the 1960s. It was not that she was making bad style choices; it was that her professional image did not match the organization she was pursuing. The hiring managers couldn't appreciate her keen engineering mind, because they couldn't look past the long, flowing skirts and beaded necklaces.

Heather was willing to modify her appearance and a year later she tried again. The new suit didn't get Heather the job, but it did allow the hiring managers to get to know Heather better, further her along in the interviewing process, and ultimately make her an offer.

Major Appearance Mistakes

Even when we pay close attention to our physical appearance, mistakes can happen. Again, we don't always see ourselves the way others do...especially when it comes to clothes. This would be a good time to bring back that "mirror, mirror on the wall".

1. Too Provocative

There needs to be a clear distinction between club clothes and work clothes. Micro-mini skirts, low-cut blouses, and exposed bra straps are not appropriate work attire. Not only is it distracting, but it's also unprofessional and can stunt your career growth. If you're wondering why your boss doesn't allow you to have face-time with clients, you might want to check your hemline.

2. Too Masculine

For a long time, as women were battling for positions in male-dominated industries, the trend was to appear more masculine. The ill-fitting pantsuits and large shoulder pads were intended to create an androgynous appearance so the focus could be on performance, not gender. It's possible, and preferable, to be a confident and successful woman while still looking like a woman.

3. Too Young

Young, and especially petite, women have an added challenge of appearing immature and lacking professional authority. It's one thing to be young chronologically; it's another thing to appear so young that others question your ability to perform your job. Look in the mirror...if you look really young and people treat you like a little girl, it's time to literally pull on the big-girl panties and make an extra effort to dress like a grown woman.

4. Too Frumpy

Some women take "business casual" to a whole new level. Even a casual work environment is still a work environment, and you should dress accordingly. Stirrup pants and maternity clothes (a year after the baby is born) say, "*I've given up on my appearance*" or "*I'm too lazy/tired to put together an appropriate outfit*". Women take care of so many people and sometimes their own physical maintenance gets forgotten. You don't have to spend a lot to look professional. Staying current on your fashion trends is just as important as staying current on your industry trends.

My Seminar and the New Mickey Mouse Club

I conducted a career transition seminar for a Fortune 500 telecommunications company for all of its laid-off employees. I was surprised to see several women in

Mickey Mouse hooded sweatshirts and made a joke about their obvious recent trip to Disney World. They looked surprised and denied any such recent trip—it was just how they all liked to dress. Being too casual can give the impression that you don't care and that you're not taking your professional responsibilities seriously. If your outfit is better suited for waiting in line for Space Mountain than it is for an office meeting, then it's time to get a new suit.

Your overall presence, how you carry yourself, and the professional image you're consciously or subconsciously creating has an enormous impact on your career. Your executive presence can say you belong either in the boardroom or the mailroom.

WOMAN UP! *Tips...*
Surprising Statistics About Your Executive Presence (EP)

1. *EP accounts for 26% of what it takes to get the next promotion.*
2. *83% of senior executives say a woman's unkempt attire detracts from her EP.*
3. *73% of senior executives say a woman's too-tight or provocative clothing detracts from her EP.*
4. *59% of senior executives say sounding uneducated detracts from a woman's EP.*
5. *28% of senior executives say communication telegraphs if you are leadership material.*

Based on a year-long study of over 4,000 college-educated professionals and 268 senior executives, conducted by Center for Talent Innovation (CTI) and in partnership with *Marie Claire* magazine.

Women, especially, pride themselves on their communication skills. We love to talk. We love to connect. We love to share. But somehow our communication skills don't always translate well into the workplace. In fact, our communication skills actually can sabotage our success.

We have spent a lot of time learning how to dress for success, but have we learned how to communicate for success? Even though verbal communication accounts for only 7% of all communication, it's powerful enough to kill our careers.

7 Verbal Miscommunication Cues

1. Using an Immature, High-Pitched Voice

It's almost impossible not to use baby talk when you actually see a new baby, but it's completely inappropriate to use that same intonation in the workplace. Studies have shown that using "baby talk" when communicating with babies and toddlers actually has a highly positive effect. There is something about the higher pitch, sing-song tone, and slower, drawn-out cadence that resonates positively with little ones.

However, it has completely the opposite effect on the grown-ups in your office. Not only does it undermine your authority and credibility as a professional woman, but it comes across as condescending and immature.

Betsy and Her Baby Talk

My client, Betsy, had a manager who would frequently use an immature tone at work. Betsy found it very difficult to respect her manager's authority and to take her seriously. She also felt like her manager was treating her like a child when she delegated assignments using a baby voice. Women will often use a high-pitched voice when they get excited or nervous. Be mindful of your tone and save the baby talk for babies.

2. Laughing When Uncomfortable

Laughing at a funny joke is one thing—laughing because you feel awkward or uncomfortable is another. Nervous laughter is a dead give-away that you lack the confidence to handle the situation. It's not always easy to mask our feelings and sometimes we can't control our reactions.

If you are one of those people, then you probably shouldn't be playing poker either. There's a reason why having a "poker face" is critical to winning the game. If you started laughing uncontrollably every time you had a straight flush or full house—or planned to bluff with a weak hand—people would know immediately and bet accordingly.

In a work environment, nervous laughter is an unprofessional big red flag and a sign of weakness. Just like the commercial, "Never let them see you sweat", the same holds true about inappropriate laughter. Exercising impulse control is an important quality in the office, especially when it comes to your verbal communication.

If you blurted out every thought that came to mind, your career would probably be short-lived. Part of being perceived as a professional woman is the ability to exhibit self-control and confidence. Outbursts of nervous laughter greatly undermine your credibility as a leader and make it hard for people to take you seriously.

3. Disguising a Strong Opinion in the Form of a Question

Women love to build consensus and to forge agreement. That strategy might work well in choosing a restaurant for dinner, but it doesn't always work well in a professional setting. Taking a stand and potentially being the minority opinion is never easy, but it's often necessary—especially when others are looking to you for expertise and leadership.

Often, women soften their opinion in the form of a question instead of speaking up with authority and ending with an exclamation point! Even if you are 100% confident in your convictions, if you end your statements with, "*Don't you think?*", "*Wouldn't you agree?*", or "*We're moving in the right direction, right?*", then you simply come across as weak and indecisive.

Heidi and Her Hesitations

My client, Heidi, was the communications director for a national non-profit company and I was brought in to help facilitate a board meeting. We started discussing the communication issues on the agenda and everyone looked to Heidi for her communications expertise, leadership, and guidance.

With every definitive opinion, Heidi always ended with a question. "I think we need to communicate better with our donors, don't you?" Then she ended another key point with, "Wouldn't it be a great idea if we updated the website?" Finally, she concluded with, "I'm sure we can all agree that consistent communication is important, right?"

Even though Heidi had all the experience and expertise she needed to make a decisive statement, she softened her remarks by couching them in the form of a question. It seriously diminished her credibility and authority and, instead, everyone overlooked Heidi and looked to the executive director to make the final decision.

4. Failing to Speak Up and Allowing Interruptions

Being seen, heard, and recognized in meetings is an important skill to master in today's business culture. Unfortunately, many women hold their tongues when they should be speaking up. Gone are the days when the teacher would call on the "quiet one" to get that student more engaged in the lesson. The onus is now on the professional to speak up and to stand out.

"We women talk too much, nevertheless we only say half of what we know."

—Nancy Witcher Astor

The problem is that people will assume you don't know anything if you don't say anything. It's not always easy to interject your ideas into a meeting filled with low, booming male voices, but sitting on your hands quietly is not an option. If people don't hear you and take notice, you're essentially invisible...and invisibility equals dispensability.

Men tend to interrupt more than women and that's a challenge, especially for women who are soft-spoken. It's easy to get railroaded and overshadowed in meetings if your message is not delivered with a loud, authoritative voice. Be bold and confident enough to hold your ground while you're speaking and don't allow anyone to interrupt you until you have finished your point.

Another roadblock for soft-spoken women is that they passively allow others to take credit for their ideas. Often when someone interrupts you, they are simply making the same point but in a much louder and more commanding tone. And then they erroneously get credit for your great idea. Intentionally or unintentionally, there are "idea thieves" in every office. Be aware.

"The most courageous act is still to think for yourself. Aloud."

—Coco Chanel

5. Using Too Many Words

Getting ahead in the business world is largely based on how well you communicate with your boss. Women, traditionally, like to communicate and express their thoughts by using an excessive amount of words. Being "too wordy" comes across as scattered and unfocused and can be an ineffective communication style when dealing with your boss.

A common communication style for men is using fewer, but well-chosen, words. They often want the "bottom line", while many women try to deliver information using the "chapter, line, and verse" method. They verbalize every single thing they're thinking and it can be confusing and misinterpreted as incompetent. Be brief, be bright, and be gone.

Lena and Her Lengthy Updates

My client, Lena, was constantly frustrated with her boss. She thought she was being thorough and thoughtful by describing every detail of the project she was managing, while her boss responded with only one-or two-word answers. He focused on the deadlines and budget and didn't want to waste time with the details. In his mind, that's why he hired Lena. By using too many words, Lena actually caused her boss to question her ability to manage the project effectively. Eventually, Lena adapted her communication style and learned how to "bottom-line" the updates for her boss.

6. Gossiping

It's not a secret that women love to share information, but it can be a slippery slope into gossiping. This is a bad habit that girls develop in high school—where it should remain after they graduate. Juicy information can be irresistible, but you need to resist it.

Knowing how important your professional brand and reputation are to your career, you never want to be known for gossiping. Being social and engaging is one thing, but be careful not to cross the line. It can cause you a lot of damage and it's a stigma that's very hard to erase. You run the risk of being viewed as untrustworthy, disloyal, and petty.

"Great minds discuss ideas, average minds discuss events, small minds discuss people."

—Eleanor Roosevelt

However, there is a big difference between knowing the office gossip and fueling the office gossip. In the interest of self-preservation and protection, you need to know what's going on, what's being said, and what's coming down the pipeline. More often than not, the gossip in the office is usually true. If you hear that your company is about to start downsizing, you need to take notice. If you hear that an advanced position is opening up, you need to take action. But there is a big difference between paying attention to what's being said and being the one to say it and spread it. Just stick to the facts.

7. Making Disclaimers

It doesn't matter if you have the most brilliant opinion or idea to contribute to the conversation if you always begin with a disclaimer. *"This may be a silly idea, but…"*, or *"I'm not sure if this is right, but…"*, or *"I don't think this will work, but…"*.

With each disclaimer you have convinced your audience that your idea is silly, is possibly wrong, and will probably not work. If the intention is to covey a powerful and confident message, nothing will undermine your authority faster than a string of disastrous disclaimers.

We focus intently on learning how to speak as toddlers, but not nearly as purposefully on what we're saying as professional adults. Words, gestures, clothing, and body language say so much about who we are, what we want, and how we're feeling. By paying attention to your communication, or miscommunication cues, you have the power to either sabotage or set yourself up for success.

⌁ Guilty Confession ⌁

I have been guilty of Miscommunication Mayhem on more than one occasion. One example that comes to mind happened early in my career. I remember being almost mute in the monthly board meetings when I worked as the advertising sales coordinator for the Chicago Bar Association. I was confident and communicative in one-on-one situations, but completely lost my voice, and subsequently my credibility, in larger groups filled with mostly male executives.

I was paralyzed with anxiety at the thought of saying the wrong thing, so I said nothing at all. I made myself completely invisible and non-existent. I worried not only about what I wanted to say, but how I was going to say it. I felt like my "friendly" tone sounded way too casual and lacked authority, while my "assertive" tone sounded like I was enraged and wanted to rip someone's head off. Because I couldn't find the right balance, I opted to say nothing at all.

Not participating and not speaking up in meetings, professional lunches, and important events really stunted my early career growth. The ironic part is that I had no trouble speaking my mind in my personal life, but struggled to find my voice in my professional life.

I am completely embarrassed to share this story, but I will, and hopefully someone will be able to relate. In my family, my grandparents would always say, *"How does that grab you?"* which really meant, *"How does that sound?"* My mistake was to bring a family colloquialism into the workplace.

I was trying to work out an issue with a guy in the accounting office at the Chicago Bar Association, and I mistakenly said, *"How does that grab you?"* He thought I said something inappropriate about "grabbing" him, and he instantly became uncomfortable and backed away from me.

I'm not sure if it was my imagination or not, but our interactions were forever awkward after that. And the more awkward I felt, the more I tried to avoid him. I never really resolved that miscommunication, but I did learn a valuable lesson—don't bring family sayings into professional conversations.

My next confession is about work attire. I am no "fashionista" and rarely follow the trends, but I always thought I looked professional and presentable. My mistake was wearing clothes that aged me well beyond my years. I was in my twenties and my sister often described my look as "Maude from the Golden Girls". Yes, that's mixing two different shows from two different eras, but the message was clear. I was dressing like a much older woman thinking that was how professional and executive women dressed. Granted it was the 90s, but that's still no excuse for gigantic shoulder pads and nude panty hose.

We are all a work in progress, and have lived through some "glamour-don't" decades, but the key is not to stay stuck wearing bright neon and sporting huge hair (ok, I still have huge hair from the 1980s...forgive me). Styles and trends evolve and so should we. If you happen to meet me, hopefully you'll notice that my professional image has drastically improved. Hopefully.

◢ Success Solutions ◣

There are so many issues to address when it comes to Miscommunication Mayhem, but there is one that shows up the most often: the inability to speak up and stand out.

When I am working with women who suffer from "soft-talking syndrome" and allow others to cut them off or interrupt them while they're speaking, there is a common theme—a lack of confidence in what they have to say compounded by having to stand up and say it in front of a room full of people. Granted, it can be nerve-wracking, but that's not a reason to avoid it. A strong presence and voice are critical to a successful career.

This is really the time to pull on those big-girl panties and *WOMAN UP!*

3 Ways to Give Your Voice Volume

1. Think Ahead
Think about the upcoming meeting or conversation and plan out what you want to say. Select at least one key point you will make that you feel really confident about, and then look at the agenda and strategically think about where and when you're going to interject that key point. If you are part of the accounting team, think about what you could add to the budget part of the conversation. If you're in marketing, think about relevant ways to contribute your ideas to the collateral brainstorming session.

2. Speak Up
Speaking up doesn't mean doing all the talking. Do your homework ahead of time and get your facts and figures together. That way you can give your input or opinion in your area of expertise with a lot more authority and confidence. You can still be selective about what you say, but you need to say something.

3. Stand Your Ground
Don't let those big personalities run you over. It's important to say something when you're interrupted or when someone is trying to take credit for your idea. Instead of either saying nothing and allowing it to happen or getting inappropriately defensive, arm yourself with some helpful phrases to combat those situations. Don't sit quietly while someone else tries to steal your thunder or sabotage your moment in the spotlight. Speak up.

WOMAN UP! *Tips...*

Helpful Phrases to Squash a Saboteur

1. *That's a great idea; we can talk about that after I'm done.*
2. *Please hold your questions and comments until I'm finished.*
3. *Excuse me, that's exactly what I just said.*
4. *You're right, that's exactly the point I'm making right now.*
5. *I didn't interrupt you when you were speaking, and I would appreciate the same courtesy.*

Finding your voice is not the only solution to Miscommunication Mayhem. Now it's time to pay attention to what you're NOT saying, but what your body language is telegraphing for you.

3 Ways to Boost Your Body Language

1. Be Aware

Think about what kind of message you're sending with your body language. Are you standing with slumped shoulders, one foot crossed in front of the other, and staring at the floor? If so, you're sending a weak, passive message. Back in the old days, girls used to walk around balancing books on their heads to ensure proper posture. Today you may get funny looks if you had a book on your head, but Emily Post had the right idea. Presence and posture say a lot about a confident woman.

2. Practice

Practice your handshake, smile, and eye contact as much as possible. Ask your honest friends and inner circle if you have a good handshake and an engaging smile; they'll tell you the truth. You only have one chance to make a positive first impression, and your handshake, smile, and eye contact speak volumes. Make it the best first impression you possibly can.

3. Model a Mentor

Whether it's verbal or non-verbal communication, modeling behaviors with a mentor is one of the best strategies to improve in these areas. A formal mentor can give you honest feedback and hold up the mirror so you can see yourself clearly. Or, identify an informal mentor to admire and to emulate (aka, professional stalking).

How does that woman handle herself in a meeting when she's interrupted? What's she wearing? How does she conduct and carry herself to earn so much respect? If you like what you see, there is no reason why you can't start adopting some of those behaviors to improve your own communication skills. It always helps to learn from the best. Steal shamelessly.

> *"We all stand on the shoulders of women who came before us. Make sure yours are strong enough to support the women who will come after you."*
>
> **—Linda Ellerbee**

WOMAN UP! power is all about women supporting other women, and not feeling unnecessarily competitive or threatened. We need to band together, pave the way, and light the path for other women to achieve their full potential. Whether it's modeling effective professional etiquette or modeling the latest professional attire...we all have the ability to be powerful role models.

◢ WOMAN UP! Reflections ◣

1. Do you suffer from "Miscommunication Mayhem"? Give an example.

   _____

   _____

   _____

   _____

   _____

   _____

2. How has it impacted your career?

   _____

   _____

   _____

   _____

   _____

   _____

   _____

3. How do you plan to change it?

   _____

   _____

   _____

   _____

   _____

   _____

UNDERVALUE EPIDEMIC

"When you undervalue what you do, the world will undervalue who you are."

—Oprah Winfrey

Undervaluing yourself is the mother of all *Deadly Sins*...and it's all about our resistance and reluctance to embrace and promote our true value. Women are a major "force" as we account for 47% of the total U.S. labor force, yet we still give our services away for free, accept less money, and downplay our value in the workplace.

Self-promotion is by far the number one issue women struggle with in my coaching practice. It's also the number one topic I'm asked to speak about to women's groups and organizations across the country.

Why is it so hard for women to toot their own horn, sing their own praises, and promote their own value?

It's because one of the first lessons we learn as little girls is that it's not polite to brag. Well, that lesson may have served us well in the sandbox and on the playground, but it doesn't serve us in a highly competitive workplace and job market.

Men, on the other hand, find it much easier to promote themselves. In fact, they are encouraged and rewarded for being competitive and aggressive. Think of Donald Trump as a living example of this unfortunate double-standard. As soon as he opens his mouth you know how much money he has, how well *The Apprentice* is doing in the ratings, the names of all his famous friends, and he finishes by asking for your vote just in case he decides to run for President.

The Disastrous "Triple-D"

For women, speaking boastfully is considered socially unacceptable, even downright rude. You will rarely hear women brag about themselves, yet they're quick to commit the ultimate self-sabotaging sin, "The Triple-D": Downplay, Dismiss, and Diminish.

WOMAN UP! *Tips...*
**You're Guilty of the "Triple-D" if You
Describe Your Success as...**

- *No big deal.*
- *It's just part of my job.*
- *Anyone could have done that.*
- *Doesn't everyone do that?*
- *Really it wasn't me, it was the whole team.*

It's bad enough that we have a hard time promoting ourselves, but we make it worse by selling ourselves short. We act as if the success never happened, or as if it were so insignificant it was hardly worth mentioning or remembering. It's even worse if someone tries to pay us a compliment or to congratulate us on a job well done. Without missing a beat, we'll deflect that compliment with some sort of self-deprecating or dismissive statement.

Gina and Her Good News

My client, Gina, worked extremely hard to become vice president of sales at a major pharmaceutical company. She was crystal-clear about the goal and committed a tremendous amount of time and energy to achieving it. The promotion was officially announced and Gina found herself extremely anxious about going to work the following day. She was equally apprehensive about the jealous jeers as she was about the well wishes.

Her strategy was to completely downplay the promotion and say, "It's really only a title change and doesn't mean anything," and then would jokingly add, "I'm sure it was a pity promotion." Achieving any goal is cause for celebration and should never be dismissed or treated as a joke.

You would never hear a male executive explain his promotion as, "I just got lucky today" or "I just happened to be in the right place at the right time." It's one thing to be humble; it's another to be inauthentic and completely downplay your own efforts that contributed to that accomplishment.

My suggestion to Gina was to practice a different response such as, "Thank you very much. It's been a goal for a long time and it feels really good to have achieved it." She immediately felt much more empowered by the words and the shift in attitude. She knew the statement was true and felt much more comfortable saying it after some additional practice. She went to work with her head held high and graciously accepted all the congratulations.

Sometimes our impulsive responses fail us and we wish we could take back what we said. Unfortunately, that's not how it works, especially in the business world. When you diminish your accomplishments, you not only do yourself an enormous disservice, but you also diminish the person giving you the compliment. Regardless of how uncomfortable you may feel when someone pays you a compliment, it's important to properly recognize that person and simply say, "*Thank you, I appreciate it.*"

Not only are women quick to dismiss a compliment, but we are also quick to undervalue our services and expertise. Women like to be of service and to be helpful to others, and the monetary reward is often lower on the priority list.

The Negotiation Game

Linda Babcock, a professor of economics at Carnegie Mellon University, conducted several studies regarding gender, money, and the power of negotiating. In one study, Babcock selected 74 volunteers to play the word game Boggle. The volunteers were told they would be paid between $3 and $10 for their time and participation. When the game was over, each volunteer was given $3 and asked if the amount was sufficient. Eight times more male volunteers than female volunteers asked for more money.

"The minute you settle for less than you deserve, you get even less than you settled for."

—Maureen Dowd

Babcock also asked students graduating with MBA degrees that had just received job offers if they tried to negotiate for more money or simply accepted the starting salary that was offered. Four times as many men—57% of men vs. 7% of women—said they negotiated for a higher salary. On average, those that negotiated received a 7% increase over the initial offer.

This amount may seem insignificant, but over time that amount adds up and makes an enormous difference. If a woman starts her career earning $25,000 and a man negotiates for a starting salary of $30,000, that man will earn approximately $361,171 more over the next 28 years than his female counterpart!

It's not that women haven't heard of negotiating, it's that we seem to avoid it like the plague. We are naturally negotiation-averse...but why?

4 Reasons Why Women Don't Negotiate

1. Too Nice

Often, women are concerned about being labeled a "bitch" and usually err so far on the other side of the pendulum that they end up being "too nice" (the "original" *Deadly Sin #1*). We are taught and conditioned to be more collaborative and less self-serving. Therefore, women tend to be less assertive when it comes to asking for what they want and what they feel they deserve.

Men seem to have an over-inflated sense of their value while women undervalue themselves. There is the same access to the market and understanding of the "going rate", but women have a harder time believing they're worth a bigger paycheck, a higher hourly rate, or a larger commission. They are more likely to "settle" than "struggle" for more money.

2. Not Motivated by Money

For a lot of women, a big paycheck is not a motivator for going to work nor is it how they measure their self-worth. Money is on the list, but it's rarely at the top of the list. They often place a much higher value on the environment, the relationships, and the intrinsic rewards of making a difference.

Women are more likely to ask for flex-time and other work accommodations to provide a greater work/life balance than they are to ask for more money. When women are married to the primary bread winner, there is even less motivation to embark on a cut-throat salary negotiation. If they don't "need" more money, it's often a battle they don't feel is worth fighting.

3. Can't Put a Price on Passion

Men are traditionally raised to be providers and, therefore, money is on their radar at a much earlier age. They will make career decisions based on salary and earning potential. Women, on the other hand, will make career decisions based on passion for a particular industry or profession.

Women already have a difficult time negotiating and promoting their value, but it's especially difficult when they LOVE what they're doing and would "do it for free". The reward is in the work and results they achieve, not in the dollar amount, and it is challenging to put a price tag on passion.

Megan and Her Medical Devices

My client, Megan, sold medical devices for many years and she loved what she did. She was very successful, consistently exceeded her sales goals, and her clients raved about her customer service. However, in Megan's opinion, she was not receiving the recognition and advancement opportunities she felt she deserved. We developed a detailed proposal she presented to her boss with all the evidence and reasons why she should be promoted.

Megan's boss was very receptive to the presentation and praised her for an outstanding job well done. He offered her the promotion, the new job title, and all the additional responsibilities that went along with it, but told her there wasn't enough money in the budget that year to increase her base salary. Megan, overjoyed by the appreciation and recognition, said "Ok" and didn't even try to negotiate.

After we debriefed from the meeting, it was painfully obvious that Megan left money on the table by quickly agreeing to the new terms and by not negotiating for more money. She said she was happy with the outcome, because she got what she wanted. Megan insisted that it "wasn't about the money" and that the recognition was the reward.

A man would never agree to do more work for the same amount of money and neither should she. My concern was that after the thrill of being put on a pedestal wore off, she would be resentful for not being appropriately compensated. Megan eventually reached the same conclusion and we strategically crafted several compensation options to present to her boss. Megan finally received not only the emotional reward she needed, but also the financial reward she deserved.

4. Take Business Personally

No one likes to hear "no" and be rejected, but that's part of doing business. Every time you embark on a negotiation you run the risk of losing and walking away empty-handed. The difference is that men don't take it as personally as women do. They can walk away, regroup, and try again another day. Men view negotiating as an exciting game to play, while women would rather have root canal surgery without anesthesia.

Women take rejection personally, as we've discussed in previous chapters. We are naturally low risk-takers, emotional beings, and perfectionists, and if the negotiation doesn't go well, we immediately assume it's our fault. The situation is designed to test our ability to separate the personal from the professional and, unfortunately, we don't always pass the test.

Denise and Her Professional Distinction

My client, Denise, had been a project manager for years. She was highly successful in that role and, therefore, her company saw no reason to make any changes. The problem was that Denise was not happy and she felt underutilized. She had outgrown the role and was interested in pursuing greater professional challenges.

The good news was that Denise knew exactly where she wanted to be—the international division of the organization—the bad news was that she had to convince her boss to approve the promotion. This meant she had to negotiate the deal, something she wasn't very confident or experienced at doing. She spent weeks preparing and practicing her presentation and was finally ready to go. However, her boss kept rescheduling the meeting.

Not only was Denise frustrated, but she took the rescheduling personally. She thought her boss was avoiding her and not taking her issue seriously. It upset Denise so much that she started questioning her ability to go through with the negotiation.

Eventually the meeting took place, Denise delivered her presentation, and her boss agreed to her promotion. Not only was Denise excited about the outcome, but she was equally proud of the way she persevered through the emotion and kept it professional.

Asking for more money or greater opportunities for ourselves can be daunting. But, somehow, we muster the courage and do it for others! Women are ruthless warriors when it comes to raising money for other people and special causes. It's interesting how we can advocate for and promote others, but have a hard time doing it for ourselves.

Maureen and Her Money

My client, Maureen, was a stay-at-home mom for years, but she hardly stayed at home. She volunteered at her children's elementary school and quickly made a name for herself. Maureen coordinated the annual auction that raised more than $100,000, convinced more than 150 local businesses to donate products and services to the event, and developed a marketing plan *that increased the auction attendance by more than 200 people.*

To pay the teacher's assistants' salaries, Maureen increased charitable donations and raised more than $50,000. She set and broke all previous donation records and was fearless in her approach to raising money for the school. Maureen was on a mission and was not going to be denied, her calls were not going to go unanswered, and the school's financial goals were not going to go unmet.

Maureen re-entered the workforce as an insurance agent and continued her winning streak of breaking and setting new records in the office. It didn't take long before she was ranked the number one agent in the office. She never took no for an answer, and had a charismatic personality that made everyone want to say yes. However, Maureen was not being adequately compensated for her performance and was not earning as much as her lesser-producing co-workers.

The obvious solution was to ask for a raise, right? After all, Maureen had a proven track record of asking for—and getting—people to give her money. But this time it wasn't for a cause, it was for herself. She battled anxiety and concern about the conversation she'd have with her boss. She thought about just letting it go. Finally, she mustered up the confidence and ultimately was successful in negotiating a raise, but her inner struggle of promoting herself and her value proved to be one of her greatest challenges.

Cathy and Her Campaign

My client, Cathy, was in a similar situation. Cathy was a highly recruited fundraiser for major non-profit organizations and political candidates. She had an innate ability to develop relationships with very wealthy and influential members of the community and to persuade them to donate to whatever cause she was promoting. She also organized spectacular events that drew unprecedented numbers of attendees and participants.

For political campaigns, she rallied constituents and enticed them to donate time and money to a particular candidate. Cathy was determined to move heaven and earth to make sure these causes and candidates were well-funded. Similar to Maureen, Cathy found herself underpaid and financially underappreciated. She literally couldn't afford to continue working and needed to earn more money. It was time to put together a campaign to raise money for her as she had done so successfully for others. Cathy's campaign produced the salary she deserved and the confidence she needed.

Whether you are promoting a cause or a candidate, women are fierce warriors for others. The same is true is in the workplace. Although you may try to downplay and dismiss your own accomplishments, you're probably more likely to promote a co-worker and sing her praises.

Amy and Her Assistant

My client, Amy, was fortunate to have an "amazing angel sent from heaven, over-qualified yet completely fulfilled, pleasure to work with everyday" type of assistant who began working for her part-time. Eventually, the assistant expressed interest in increasing the position to full-time. Not wanting the assistant to look elsewhere, Amy launched a full-blown campaign to help her assistant achieve full-time status that included extensive strategic planning, numerous letters of recommendation, documented accomplishments, and an endless list of added-value elements this assistant brought to the table. Amy went to war for her assistant and left no stone unturned, no conversation unspoken, no objection unresolved, and her assistant received her full-time promotion.

Amy was a gladiator in the work arena, but it was for someone else. Would she have been as courageous and bold if it was for herself? Why are we more willing to go out on a limb to promote someone else while we stay safely on the ground?

Not only are we more willing to speak up for someone else, but we're also more likely to speak up *somewhere* else. We assertively ask for what we want in restaurants, stores, and schools, but not in the workplace. As consumers we exercise our buying power and make sure we get exactly what we want. Women want value and we know how to get it.

"It's never too late to become the person you have always wanted to be."

—Anne Sweeney

There is a very memorable diner scene in the 1989 movie, *When Harry Met Sally* (no, not *that* scene, but close!), that illustrates this conundrum perfectly. Harry and Sally are sitting in a diner placing their orders with a very patient server. Harry easily orders off the menu and then it is Sally's turn. If you recall the scene, Sally wants a simple piece of pie, but her ordering of the pie is anything but simple.

Sally requests numerous variations of toppings and insists everything be served "on the side". Clearly, she was a woman who knew exactly what she wanted and was not going to settle for anything less. Sally wasn't concerned about being perceived as a bitch, and didn't care if the server found her to be bossy or controlling.

The real question becomes, would Sally have been as confident to state her demands at work? Would she have negotiated for the corner office with a company car and new assistant "on the side"?

So strong is our aversion to negotiating at work that many of my clients have contemplated looking for another job rather than asking for a raise, promotion, or transfer to another department. Granted it's an uncomfortable and potentially awkward conversation, but it's made worse by the fact that women negotiate so infrequently. It's just like any skill—if you don't use it, you lose it.

In one study conducted by the Harvard Business School in 2003, several hundred people were surveyed over the internet. The respondents were asked "about the most recent negotiations they'd attempted or initiated and when they expected to negotiate next". The study showed that men place themselves in negotiation situations more often than women do and regard more of their interactions as potential negotiations.

Self-promotion and negotiation don't come naturally to many of us, which is why it's critical we practice and gain more confidence in those areas. If you never ask for what you want and celebrate your successes, it would be like expecting to speak a foreign language without learning a single word. It's time to flex that self-promotion muscle and get it in tip-top shape. We already know that the muscle is strong enough to promote other people and other causes, but are YOU ready to stop settling for less, accepting less than you deserve, and selling yourself short? *WOMAN UP!* Step up and stand out.

───

⬧ Guilty Confession ⬧

This is my worst *Deadly Sin*...and I coach women on self-promotion every day. Yikes!

For instance, I was nominated for the Outstanding Women in Business award by the *Denver Business Journal* and I wasn't going to mention it to anyone besides my husband. I actually convinced myself that it was "no big deal" and wasn't worth bothering anyone with the news.

I happened to see another nominee announce her good news on LinkedIn and I felt like a complete fool. She was promoting herself, like a smart business woman should, and so should I. I pulled on my big-girl panties and posted my good fortune on social media and the support and well wishes were overwhelming. No one felt "bothered" by the news. Instead, they were genuinely happy for me. Lesson learned…hopefully!

Like so many of my clients, I have no trouble promoting other people. In fact, I love sharing great news and congratulating clients and colleagues on a job well done. I'm just not always as excited to acknowledge or share my own great news.

I am also guilty of deflecting compliments. It's horrible and I know my responses should be better. Just like I coach my clients to simply say, "*Thank you*", I can't quite seem to take my own advice. This may sound like a silly example, but people have been complimenting me on my crazy, curly hair for my entire life. I don't quite understand the fascination and awe over my unruly mane, so my honest response is usually, "*Uuughhh, it's the bane of my existence (which is true)!*" The person usually walks away feeling totally dejected and I feel even worse. It's time for me to master the "*Thank you*" response.

However, my worst sin in this category has to be my constant battle with value and pricing my services and expertise in the marketplace. I absolutely love what I do and "would do it for free", like many women who are fortunate to love their work. Unfortunately, loving what you do so much you'd give it away for free does not always make the best business model.

For years, I would feely give advice to job seekers in desperate need of information to help with their job search. It was incredibly rewarding knowing I was helping someone in need, but it was not helping me financially. I have delivered more free presentations than I care to remember, and usually said "yes" to whatever measly dollar amount someone offered to pay me. Pitiful, right?

I rationalized the "free" presentations as a clever marketing strategy. Even though it did increase my visibility and credibility among job seekers and gained new clients with every presentation, the reality was that I didn't have enough confidence to negotiate a reasonable fee and dreaded hearing the word "no". I didn't realize that 100% of what you don't ask for, you don't get. I didn't ask for a fee, and therefore I didn't get one. What a surprise!

It took a long time, and remains a constant focus, for me to claim my value and believe I'm worth more money. When I started my consulting business in 1995, my fees were laughably low, but again I rationalized it as my "start-up rate" and promised to increase my rates as I gained experience and perfected my processes. I had the best of intentions, but it took years before I had enough courage to ask for more money. The funny thing is that after I finally raised my rates, no one ever complained or questioned the new pricing structure, and I felt like a fool for not doing it sooner.

I was coaching clients successfully every day on how to negotiate and ask for more money, but I was completely paralyzed at the prospect of doing it for myself. I related to my clients struggling with claiming their own value, and knew on a very deep, personal level how important it was to finally conquer those fears. To some degree, I was trying to learn the lesson as I was teaching the lesson. The teacher definitely became the student.

I doubled my rates a short time after that and, even though I'm probably considered a bargain in the consulting world, I can confidently stand behind my new prices and know I'm worth every penny and more. I no longer negotiate or reduce my rates and I rarely give anything away for free. It's about progress, not perfection, and I'm always a work in progress when it comes to self-promotion and value.

◢ Success Solutions ◣

The Undervalue Epidemic is one of the hardest sins to cure and sabotages the most careers. If you don't know how to ask for what you want and negotiate what you rightfully deserve, you'll never reach your true professional potential.

The first step is to believe you have value, bring value, and are valuable. If you don't believe it with every fiber of your being, no one else will either. It may take some time, and you may need someone else to hold up the mirror to help you see your value, but it's worth it.

The goal is not to negotiate like a ruthless shark; the goal is to really understand your value, become more assertive, and go after what you want versus merely accepting what's offered to you. It may not happen overnight, but it will happen with some practice and a heavy dose of confidence...this is really where the big-girl panties come in handy. *WOMAN UP!* and finally graduate from negotiation denial to negotiation dynamo.

12 Tips to Transform Negotiating Skills

1. Be Yourself

Learning to become better at negotiating doesn't mean that you need to learn to become a different person. It's about learning to become a more assertive and self-confident version of yourself.

Nothing is more off-putting for a hiring manager than to get to know and to come to like a candidate during the hiring process, only to discover that her evil, alter-ego shows up for the salary negotiation. No one likes to feel blindsided and misled—especially a hiring manager.

Stay true to yourself, your personality, your values, and your integrity, even in a negotiation. It's about improving your negotiating skills, not playing Jekyll and Hyde.

2. Get a Goal

The most important thing to know about negotiating is that it needs to have a purpose. What's the goal? What are you trying to achieve? What's your intention? What does a successful outcome look like?

You can negotiate a raise, a starting salary, a promotion, a business partnership, or a client contract, but without identifying the goal, it's nearly impossible to put together an action plan to get you there. Negotiation needs direction and focus in order to be effective. Otherwise, it's bluster without benefit.

3. Know Your Bottom Line

Now that you know the goal, it's time to know your bottom line. How low will you go? What conditions will you accept? What conditions will you not accept? What's your "walk-away" price? You should know what you're willing to give up or sacrifice before coming to the negotiating table.

If you're negotiating to work remotely three days a week to achieve a greater work/life balance, would you accept two days a week? If you're negotiating a starting salary and it's your dream job, would you accept $5,000 less to secure the offer? If you're a consultant and your client wants to negotiate a better rate in exchange for a longer contract, would you agree?

Knowing your bottom line before the negotiation even begins provides better boundaries and structure and reduces the chances of you saying "yes" when you really should be saying "no".

4. Be Realistic

A big part of a successful negotiation is setting realistic expectations. Do your homework ahead of time, research the industry, and understand the current market conditions and extenuating circumstances.

If a starting salary reflects the "going rate" of $50,000, then asking for $100,000 may not work. Or, if you're trying to hire additional employees during a "hiring freeze", understand that you're likely to be turned down.

You want to set yourself up for success when it comes to negotiating, and a big part of that is establishing realistic expectations. Know that a "yes" is even a possibility before you ask the question.

5. Script it Out

Knowing what you want to say ahead of time, planning it out, and practicing helps keep the mind from going blank. Or worse, saying the wrong thing. Confidence is such a critical component to negotiating and nothing kills confidence faster than a blank mind or the wrong word(s). Actors use a script... why shouldn't you?

Think about the negotiation as a presentation with a beginning, middle, and a successful end. Script it out, choose your words carefully, and practice delivering the presentation in front of a trusted friend or colleague. This will help calm your nerves when it's finally "show time".

6. Anticipate Objections

Brainstorming ahead of time of every conceivable reason why the other person would say "no" is critical to a negotiation. Not only does your ability to overcome the objections boost your chances of hearing a "yes", but it instantly boosts your confidence.

If you're asking for a promotion, think about why your boss would deny your request. Play devil's advocate. Would he/she say you need more experience? An advanced degree? Or stronger leadership skills? Then, plan out what you will say in return. Don't be defensive, but counter constructively with facts. How you handle yourself in these pressure situations will often determine the outcome of a negotiation.

Anticipating the objections ahead of time, and practicing an appropriate response, reduces the likelihood of getting blindsided or derailed during a negotiation. You never want to be caught off-guard. A flustered negotiator usually walks away empty-handed.

7. Bring Alternatives

Of course you always want to come prepared with your first choice, your ideal outcome, but what about a second and third choice? If the goal is to create a win-win situation and seal the deal, then you want to provide options for the other person. Do some creative thinking beforehand so you don't leave the negotiating table without a signed contract.

When our realtor was selling our home, she got extremely creative. Of course our first choice was to get the full asking price, but if that wasn't going to happen she sweetened the deal with other incentives. The second choice was the full asking price plus a membership to the community pool. The third choice was the full asking price plus the pool membership and a year of free lawn service. The third choice was the charm, and the negotiation was complete.

Walking in with only one option is too limiting for a negotiation. It creates an all-or-nothing situation. Working together to find a suitable solution is always in your best interest. In every negotiation, the parties each need to feel as if they've won something. Bring alternatives and walk out a winner.

8. Avoid Emotion

Even though you may be emotionally invested in the outcome of the negotiation, you can't show the emotion during the negotiation. This is the time to put on your poker face, otherwise you risk losing your negotiating power and credibility. Remember, it's about resolving a mutual problem, not about the people involved or their feelings.

If you're at the final stage of the interviewing process, and the hiring manager can sense your desperation, your opportunity to negotiate a higher starting salary just passed. It's easier said than done, but negotiating is the time to stay calm and to keep your cool. If you show up angry, anxious, or teary-eyed, you can kiss your negotiating power goodbye.

9. Practice Makes Perfect

Instead of waiting to negotiate a raise once a year, look for other opportunities to negotiate and assert yourself on a more regular basis. If you only go to the gym once a year, of course you'll be disappointed with the results. It doesn't work.

Negotiating is a muscle that needs constant exercise. Go to the flea market or a yard sale and negotiate a better price on a crappy candle stick. If it works out, great, but if not, all you lost out on was a crappy candle stick. You were assigned a middle seat on your cross-country flight, so ask to be moved to an aisle seat or first-class because you're a frequent flyer. Your steak arrived well-done after you ordered it medium-rare, so send it back until the steak is done to your liking.

Learn how to ask for what you want, negotiate what you need, and walk away if it doesn't work out. If you exercise that assertive muscle more often, then it will be strong and ready when you need it.

10. Seek Support

It takes a village to raise a child, and sometimes it also takes a village to build up an assertive woman. You may not have been born with a strong backbone, but you can strengthen the one you have with help and support.

Whether it's a work BFF who encourages you to "go for it" or a wise mentor who helps you think it through, gathering support before, during, and after a nerve-wracking negotiation is often the confidence you need to be more assertive.

Rallying support and announcing your intentions is an effective way to create accountability. If you tell your friends you're trying to lose 10 pounds, you know someone will ask how your diet is going. That accountability is often the gentle nudge we need to negotiate a new contract, ask for more money, or lose weight.

11. Think of a Third Person

If you still find it painfully difficult to negotiate for yourself, then think about who else would benefit from your successful negotiation. Remember, we're unstoppable when it comes to advocating, helping, and supporting others.

Perhaps your ailing spouse would be better off if you negotiated better healthcare benefits, your son could attend college out of state if you negotiated a higher raise, or you could visit your family more often if you negotiated for more vacation time.

Thinking about how a negotiation could help someone else is often the incentive we need to pull on those big-girl panties and negotiate like a pro.

12. Celebrate Success

Celebrating successes of all sizes is critical to overall career success. If you try to negotiate a raise for the first time ever, celebrate the fact that you stepped outside your comfort zone regardless of the outcome. Positive reinforcement increases the likelihood that you'll take another, perhaps greater risk in the future.

If you asked for a $10,000 raise, but only got $5,000, celebrate that fact that you're still making more money than you did last year. If you negotiated for a higher starting salary, but instead they offered you more vacation time, celebrate the fact that you're beginning a new job in two weeks and starting thinking about how you'll enjoy that extra time off.

"Embrace change. Don't let fear of the unknown impede your personal and professional growth."

—Larree Renda

Can you apply these 12 tips? Of course! And one more piece of advice: don't be afraid of asking. Practice your negotiating skills in all areas of your life. Try out new techniques and see what works or learn from someone who's had success. Review your performance and plan how to approach the next negotiation. Preparation is the key. Then, celebrate the progress you've made and the results you've achieved rather than lamenting what you've lost. If you treat a negotiation as an all-or-nothing, do-or-die, complete-success or utter-failure situation, of course you'll be less likely to dip your toe in the negotiating pool next time.

♦ WOMAN UP! Reflections ♦

1. Are you suffering from the "Undervalue Epidemic"? Give an example.

    _____

    _____

    _____

    _____

    _____

    _____

2. How has it impacted your career?

    _____

    _____

    _____

    _____

    _____

    _____

3. How do you plan to change it?

    _____

    _____

    _____

    _____

    _____

    _____

Conclusion
FROM SIN TO SUCCESS

"No matter who you are, no matter what you did, no matter where you've come from, you can always change, become a better version of yourself."

—Madonna

N ow we know we're raging perfectionists who suffer from the disease to please, require constant adulation, and talk too much while giving all our services and expertise away for free. So, now what? How can we *WOMAN UP!* and achieve the success we deserve?

Onward and Upward

When it comes to making meaningful changes in our lives, the first step is to recognize what needs to be changed. If any of the *Deadly Sins* resonated with you, if any of the client stories sounded far too familiar, or if you connected with any of my own guilty confessions, then it's time to step up, take action, and catapult yourself onward and upward.

You are already an amazing, talented, and inspiring woman who's just as imperfect as the rest of us. We are incredibly powerful beings capable of accomplishing more than we ever imagined. If we can rule a country, conquer cancer, and lovingly lead a family, then we can definitely turn these *Deadly Sins* and self-sabotaging behaviors into success stories.

Remember, you already have a solid foundation, a nearly-complete outfit. Now it's time to take a good, hard look in the mirror to see if any of these *Deadly Sins* are holding you back. Are there any "successories" you can add that will take your career to the next level? Are there modifications you can make that will make an enormous difference in your career? Have you identified a destructive pattern of behavior that you'd like to change? Are you ready to stop living the definition of insanity and try something new?

If, Then…

If you're tired of always being ***too kind***, then it's time to curb the ***conundrum*** and stop apologizing.

If you're exhausted from being ***too competent,*** then it's time to break the ***curse*** by learning how to say "no" and mean it.

If you're frustrated by trying to be **too perfect**, then it's time to bust out of that **prison** and burn that bridge.

If you're suffering from needing **too much affirmation**, then it's time to end the **addiction** and become your own BFF.

If you're **too divulging,** then it's time to cure the **disease** and think before you speak, post, and share.

If you're guilty of **too much miscommunication,** then it's time to manage the **mayhem** and understand what your words and body language are really saying.

If you're struggling with being **too undervalued,** then it's time to stop the **epidemic** and learn how to negotiate with power.

"Sometimes, the best way to make a big difference is adding up lots of small ones."

—Queen Rania Al Abdullah of Jordan

Rome wasn't built in a day and significant change doesn't happen overnight. It's about asking the right questions, accepting the honest feedback, making brave choices, and committing to taking action. It's not about blaming yourself, punishing yourself, or trying to turn yourself into someone you're not.

By making strategic improvements in how you conduct yourself in the workplace, you ultimately get to live as the best version of yourself. You will achieve goals that may have previously been out of reach. You will enter conversations that may have previously been closed. And, you will optimize opportunities that may have been unavailable previously.

Because "she who dies with the least amount of regrets wins", this really is a competition worth winning. If you aggressively apply for a new job even though you only match 85% of the job description, you win. If you successfully refrain from gossiping at the office, you win. If you boldly negotiate a raise for yourself, you win.

Even though an Olympic athlete has the raw talent to win most competitions, she still needs to look within and see where she can make improvements. Maybe she needs to change her nutrition, sleep habits, or training techniques. If the goal is to win the gold medal, then she'll do whatever it takes.

The same is true in the workplace. If you already possess the raw materials (intelligence, drive, skills, experience, etc.), but you continuously take home the silver medal, then it's time to look within. What do you need to do to avoid self-sabotaging behavior and set yourself up for even greater success? What "successories" can you add to complete your portfolio?

"When you feel hopeless and decide not to go, fight that dragon. Chest out, pumps on, out the door woman."
—Giselle Fernandez

Whether you find a mentor, take a risk, or exercise greater impulse control on social media the message is the same... the power lies within. You may need help and support from external sources, but just like Dorothy with her ruby slippers, you already have the power to take yourself wherever you want to go. But you have to take action and click your stiletto heels to take flight.

The Self-Confidence Cure

The *Deadly Sins* are only deadly if you allow them to be, and they all have one cure in common...self-confidence. Self-confidence gives you the boost you need to say "no" when you normally say "yes". It gives you the power to stop a saboteur from interrupting your presentation. And it gives you the strength you need to increase your monetary value.

With a healthy dose of confidence, none of the self-sabotaging behaviors have a snowball's chance of surviving a hot summer day. Confidence is the foundation upon which all else is built. So, what does it take to be a confident woman today? If you look at highly successful and confident women, they share a lot of similar qualities.

> Woman UP! *Tips...*
> **12 Qualities of Highly Confident Women**
>
> 1. *They don't feel threatened, only inspired.*
> 2. *They shine the spotlight on others and celebrate their success.*
> 3. *They listen more than they speak.*
> 4. *They surround themselves with other brilliant women.*

5. *They don't throw others under the bus in order to look good.*

6. *They realize when they need help and ask for it.*

7. *They embrace their femininity and don't try to be men.*

8. *They are not afraid to look silly or be wrong.*

9. *They own their mistakes and move on.*

10. *They don't try to please everyone, only those that matter.*

11. *They trust their instincts and intuition.*

12. *They believe they are worthy of success and good fortune.*

Confidence is not something you're born with, it's something you build. It's something you work on and cultivate throughout your life. Every time you overcome an obstacle, you build confidence. Every time you rise to meet a new challenge, you build confidence. Every time you fail but persist, you build confidence. And every time you win, you build confidence.

As adults, we have a tendency to get comfortable and complacent. We need to remember that exuberant feeling of accomplishment and actively seek out greater challenges. Instead of shying away, we need to pull on those big-girl panties and say *"I can do it!"* (or at least, *"I'll give it a try!"*).

With a little confidence, you might say "yes" to a project unlike anything you've done before, agree to deliver a presentation to an audience larger than you've ever seen, or manage a conflict you've never encountered before. With every new experience, with every new step, you gain more and build more confidence.

The problem is that we don't always remember those moments of greatness that boost our confidence. The negative inner dialogue and daily mini-dramas seem to scream louder and demand our attention, while the highlights and "job well done" accolades fade into oblivion. It's like the child who gets immediate attention by throwing a full-blown tantrum, while the well-behaved child sits quietly waiting to be acknowledged.

When it comes to consciously elevating your self-confidence and mastering the art of tooting your own horn, there is one tip that works like a charm every time. It is perhaps the easiest action step to take and it will have the greatest impact on your ability to *WOMAN UP!* It's called a "Brag Book".

What is a "Brag Book"? A "Brag Book" is an ongoing and fully updated log or record of all your accomplishments, achievements, and successes. The "Brag Book" rules are simple, but the benefits are enormous.

WOMAN UP! *Tips...*
"Brag Book" Rules and Benefits

Rules:
1. *The Brag Book is a journal, notebook, folder, and/ or file.*
2. *The Brag Book lives at home!*
3. *The Brag Book gets updated every week or every two weeks.*

4. *The Brag Book ONLY contains positive information!*
5. *The Brag Book contains successes of ALL sizes...no judgment.*

Benefits:

1. *It helps to have that information ready to update your résumé.*
2. *It helps to have that information ready for performance reviews.*
3. *It means you don't have to rely on your memory.*
4. *It counterbalances the tendency to downplay, dismiss, and diminish.*
5. *It boosts your confidence and empowers you to WOMAN UP!*

A "Brag Book" is a tangible reminder, and record-keeper, of all you have accomplished. It can include raving emails from clients, positive performance reviews, innovative templates you created, awards and promotions, letters of recommendation, rankings, results from completing a project on time and under budget, processes you improved that made or saved the company money, or a newspaper clipping with a quote from you.

Instead of constantly feeling like you're searching for this elusive self-confidence to magically appear one day, start making it happen. Stop denying your successes and start owning them. An updated "Brag Book" is that sacred space where you are only allowed to celebrate your successes, savor your accomplishments, and build the self-confidence that every woman needs.

Self-confidence enables you to slay the sins and take control over your career. Throughout your career there will be people and politics you can't control, so why not focus on what you *can* control? You can control how much information you share with co-workers, how many opportunities you let pass by because they're not perfect enough, and how much energy you expend worrying if other people like you. When it comes to self-confidence, there is always room for improvement.

Don't allow limiting beliefs and a lack of awareness to sabotage your career any longer. Take control and squash the *7 Deadly Sins* once and for all. These are life lessons we can learn from, triumph over, and use to catapult us to unimaginable success. Slide into those steel stiletto heels and send the message that you will not be denied.

WOMAN UP! is not just the title of this book…it is a power trip in the best possible way. It is my intention that it becomes a movement. It becomes a rallying cry for all women to dig deep, discover their inner strength, and celebrate their beauty and power. It becomes a shout of encouragement and a sign of support from one woman to another. "*WOMAN UP! because I know you can do it and I have your back.*"

So, motivate yourself with plenty of *WOMAN UP!* power before that important meeting, job interview, or crucial conversation. Inspire the women in your life with a *WOMAN UP!* cheer when they need a lift. And reward yourself with a congratulatory *WOMAN UP!* high-five for a job well done.

Thank you for taking this personal journey with me into the world of empowering women to realize and reach their full professional potential. I do it every day with great pride and tremendous passion, and I am constantly amazed, and in awe, of the true power we possess. I hope you feel inspired and motivated to exceed your own expectations...and I hope you find it within yourself to *WOMAN UP!*

ABOUT THE AUTHOR

If you want to know Aimee Cohen, then you need to know what she believes: *"There is a special place in hell for women who don't help other women."* (Madeleine Albright)

Aimee Cohen is a Career Expert, Author, and Keynote Speaker. She owns Cohen Career Consulting, is a contributing writer for the *Denver Business Journal*, facilitates the LINK to Leadership program for the Leadership Investment, has appeared as a career expert on Denver's *Channel 7* and *Channel 4 News*, has been interviewed on several radio shows, has been cited in *Glamour* magazine and the *Denver Post*, was featured in *Denver Woman* magazine, and received recognition as an *Outstanding Women in Business Award* nominee,

With a nearly 100% success rate, Aimee enables women to implement a strategic step-by-step action plan with proven techniques that generate results. Aimee's approach, methodology, and message are all about empowerment, encouragement, and action...it's not only informational, it's transformational. She's a realist with vision, but her real gift lies in her ability to empower women to realize and reach their full professional potential and gain the confidence they need to exceed their own expectations.

For more than 20 years, she has coached hundreds of clients in personalized one-on-one consultations, led outplacement transition seminars for *Fortune 500* companies, and delivered dynamic presentations to audiences of all sizes. Aimee specializes in keynote speeches targeting women's groups, organizations, and associations. She has been specifically brought in to address gender issues and inequalities that can exist in male-dominated industries such as government, oil and gas, and higher education.

Aimee grew up in Evanston, Illinois, and graduated with a B.A. in Political Science from the University of Michigan. She has lived in Denver, Colorado, since 1993 with her husband Adam (a passionate, expert performance excellence catalyst), son Zachary (a Cadet at the United States Military Academy at West Point), daughter Rachel (a top-ranked rock climber, terrific student, and independently driving sophomore in high school), and a loving yellow lab, Rosie.

Find out more about Aimee at
www.womanuppower.com
or follow her at
@womanuppower.

Join the WOMAN UP!
community at
www.facebook.com/womanuppower.

ACKNOWLEDGMENTS

They say it takes a village to raise a child. For me, it has taken a universe to write this book. Not only do I have an endless list of champions and cheerleaders to thank, but I also have a lifetime of trials and tribulations to appreciate.

I would like to thank my family first. My husband, Adam, who met me before I was born (literally!) and has seemingly loved me my whole life. Not only has he heard all my stories, but has lived most of them with me. I thank you for your strength, your patience, your unconditional love, and for giving me the greatest adventure of my life...our family.

I also need to thank you for singlehandedly being my entire support staff: IT department, editor, designer, business administrator, and task master. You have kept me sane, made me laugh, and never gave up on me. But most of all, thank you for having the guts to tell me to *WOMAN UP!* when I needed it the most.

To my children, Zachary and Rachel, I want to thank you for not caring whether I finished this book or not, was a successful career coach or not, or made millions of dollars or not. To you, I'm just Mom...and that will forever be my greatest accomplishment and the title I cherish the most. You fill my heart with more love and pride than I ever knew existed. You fill my days with more laughter and joy than I ever imagined. And you fill my life with more purpose and meaning than I ever dreamed possible.

Thank you to my lovingly blended family: Mom, Michael, Dad, Julie, Gabriel, Becky, Adam, Joshua, Hannah, and Jake. Somehow we found a way to make it all work and for that I am grateful. Thank you for your love and support.

Thank you to my grandparents who are no longer with us, but who are always with me. You helped me find my first empty desk and always believed in me. You were always my greatest advocates and the strongest supporters in my life. You filled your home with an abundance of laughter and unconditional love, and I have proudly and graciously carried that legacy into my home. You are deeply missed.

My story, and this book, would not have been possible without recognizing some very significant people in my life. Thank you, David Beam and Thomas Peay, two of the kindest and most compassionate men you'll ever meet. They believed in me early in my career when I did not, and each possessed the wherewithal to ask me my favorite interviewing question and to give me a chance. Thank you both from the bottom of my heart.

Thank you to Kristen Moeller, my writing coach extraordinaire. The universe sent you to me just when I needed you. Thank you for your words of wisdom, inspiration, and encouragement and for telling me what I needed to hear instead of what I wanted to hear. I know, in the deepest part of myself, that I would not have finished this book without you. Thank you.

Even though it's important to be your own BFF (see *Deadly Sin #4*), it's even more important to appreciate the kick-ass, loyal-to-the-end girlfriends who make your life (and book) possible. Thank you to Deb Chromik, Melissa Cook, Laura Dean, Molly Gibson, Betsy Keyes, Mindy Serota, Darcy Sherman, Lynne Valencia, and Irene Zimmer for being constant sources of inspiration and for giving me the strength and confidence to go the distance. Thank you for providing honest feedback and brilliant suggestions, for making me laugh and cry, for demonstrating what it's like to triumph over adversity, and for picking me up when I'm down. You are all living, shining examples of what it means to *Woman Up!*

I need to send a huge thank you to all my clients over the last 20 years. You have enriched my life beyond words, and have taught me lessons I didn't even know I needed to learn. I have felt your pain, embraced your struggles, and celebrated your successes. Your journey has been my journey, and I have loved and appreciated every single moment. I may not have been born a career coach, but I was born to BE a career coach, and I can honestly say it's been rewarding and fulfilling beyond my wildest dreams. Thank you all for your trust, your confidence, your hard work, and your stories.

Finally, I'd like to recognize and thank my many formal and informal mentors. You have all been gracious and generous, and I still hang on your every word and take everything you say to heart. You are self-made, successful women and true role models. I love your wit, honesty, and chutzpah. I have plenty of wit and honesty, but could certainly turn up the chutzpah and *WOMAN UP!*

ARE YOU READY TO *WOMAN UP!* ?

Keynote Speaking

Aimee Cohen motivates and compels action through practical and inspiring keynote speeches and breakout presentations—always customized and targeted to meet the unique needs of the groups and individuals.

She has addressed and provided workshops for groups of all sizes and in all segments, including government, non-profit, higher education, and the private sector.

Invite her to address your women's group, professional association, company, division, or team.

Workshops

If your group is ready to pull on those big-girl panties, dig deep, and work on strategies to overcome the *7 Deadly Sins* (and other challenges women face!), a customized workshop is your ticket to success. From half-and single-day seminars to multi-day workshops, let Aimee Cohen guide your team to the success you want and deserve.

Merchandise

Promote your pride or motivate yourself with merchandise emblazoned with the *WOMAN UP!* call to action. Reward and inspire your family, friends, and your co-workers for a job well done with fun items.

Book Copies

Supply your team, big or small, with more copies of *WOMAN UP!* Start a book club at work or in the community. Or, offer the book as a gift to clients, colleagues, and co-workers. It's a combination of your best girlfriend and an elite career expert in a powerful, purse-sized package.

For more information, visit www.womanuppower.com.

REFERENCES

Deadly Sin #1

Schumann, Karina, and Michael Ross. "Why Women Apologize More Than Men: Gender Differences in Thresholds for Perceiving Offensive Behavior." *Psychology Science* 11 (2010):1649-55.

Deadly Sin #2

Avon Products, Inc. "Avon Mentoring Matters Survey". 1998.

American Society for Training & Development. "2013 State of the Industry Report." Alexandria: ASTD. 2013.

Tyler, K. "Mentoring Programs Link Employees and Experienced Execs." *HR Magazine* 43 (1998): 98-103.

Deadly Sin #3

American Society of Plastic Surgeons. *"2012 Plastic Surgery Statistics Report."* http://www.plasticsurgery.org/news/plastic-surgery-statistics.html.

Szymanski, Jeff, Ph.D. *The Perfectionist's Handbook: Take Risks, Invite Criticism, and Make the Most of Your Mistakes.* Hoboken: John Wiley and Sons, 2011.

Domar, Alice, Ph.D., "Why Do Women Need To Be Perfect?" *TIME.* April 21, 2008.

Schnall, Simone, et al. "Social Support and the Perception of Geographical Slant." *Journal of Experimental Social Psychology* 44 (2008): 1246–1255.

Deadly Sin #5

International Listening Association, http://www.listen.org/research.

Harris Interactive and CareerBuilder. "More Employers Finding Reasons Not to Hire Candidates on Social Media." June 27, 2013. http://www.careerbuilder.com/Share/AboutUs/PressReleases.aspx?archiveyear=2013.

Deadly Sin #6

Carney, Dana R., Amy J.C. Cuddy, and Andy J. Yap. "Power Posing: Brief Nonverbal Displays Affect Neuroendocrine Levels and Risk Tolerance." *Psychological Science* 21 (2010): 1363–1368.

Hewlett, S.A., et al. "Executive Presence." New York: Center for Talent Innovation, 2012.

Deadly Sin #7

Babcock, Linda, and Sara Laschever. *Women Don't Ask: Negotiation and the Gender Divide.* Princeton: Princeton University Press, 2003.

Babcock, Linda, Sara Laschever, Michele Gelfand, and Deborah Small. "Nice Girls Don't Ask." *Harvard Business Review*, October 1, 2003.

CPSIA information can be obtained at www.ICGtesting.com
Printed in the USA
LVOW13s0532300414

383787LV00004B/7/P